ADA®

An Introduction
Second Edition—January 1983

by Henry Ledgard

Springer-Verlag
New York Heidelberg Berlin

ADA® is a registered trademark of the U.S. Government ADA Joint Program Office

Henry Ledgard
Drummer Hill Road
Leverett, MA 01054
U.S.A.

Library of Congress Cataloging in Publication Data
Ledgard, Henry F., 1943–
    Ada, an introduction
    Includes index.
    1. Ada (Computer program language) I. Title.
QA76.73.A35L42   1982   001.64′24   82-19444

ADA® is a registered trademark of the U.S. Government ADA Joint
Program Office.

Printed and bound by Halliday Lithograph, West Hanover,
Massachusetts.
Printed in the United States of America.

9 8 7 6 5 4 3 2 1

ISBN 0-387-90814-5 Springer-Verlag New York Heidelberg Berlin
ISBN 3-540-90814-5 Springer-Verlag Berlin Heidelberg New York

PREFACE

If Charles Babbage is to be regarded as the father of modern day computer technology, then surely the Countess Augusta Ada Lovelace, after whom this new language is named, must be remembered as its midwife.

It was she, the daughter of England's poet Lord Byron, who translated the work of the Italian mathematician L.F. Menabrea, attaching her own scientific commentaries on the dissimilarities between the difference engine and the analytical engine. It was Lady Lovelace, the great lady of computers, who delivered the notes and loosely organized writings of Babbage, with her own invaluable amendments, to a world not quite ready to receive them.

The Ada language effort has employed hundreds, if not thousands, of minds and a healthy sum of money since its conception. Ada was fostered by the High Order Language Working Group (HOLWG), chartered by the U.S. Department of Defense in January of 1975 with the overall objective of developing a systematic approach to improved use of software by the military.

One would think the Pentagon an unlikely foster parent for a new computer language. Regardless of its lineage, the question that begs asking is, of course — Why? The answer is by no means a simple one, but some brief background may help to clarify the matter.

At present, the Department of Defense is the largest software consumer on earth, employing roughly 400 different computer languages and dialects. The situation, some have commented, is at best untidy.

The bulk of this rhetoric, and over half the cost of maintaining it, is to be found in "embedded computer systems" — those systems that are part of a larger, electromechanical arrangement. Examples are found in sophisticated weaponry, aircraft, ships, spacecraft, a rapid transit network, or a message switching system. The outputs are the familiar computer control signals and data sheets. An embedded computer system is the computer within a device, the ubiquitous agent behind the scene that makes things happen.

Given the vastness and diversity of this machinery, a logical panacea would be a universal computer tongue. The most visible output of the High Order Language Working Group was a series of reports documenting the technical prerequisites for such a language. Each report generated considerable interest by persons both inside and outside of the Department of Defense. The entire matter was thought, rethought, rethought again, and finally boiled down to another edition. These papers became known as the Strawman, Woodenman, Tinman, Ironman, Revised Ironman, and ultimately Steelman.

During this process, the idea of a common computer language gained momentum. It was not only felt to be a desirable goal, but also feasible. Technical analysis, coupled with political pressures from all sides, ruled out the idea of adopting an existing language. It was only a matter of time before the Department of Defense put the development of this new departure out to bid.

That came in Spring of 1977. Some 17 organizations submitted proposals, and within a few months, four of these were selected to prepare an initial design. Thus began, in the entire history of computer languages, the first major language design competition.

The four finalists were Softech and Intermetrics, both of Massachusetts,

SRI International from California, and the Honeywell affiliate Cii Honeywell Bull of France. By March of 1978 the candidates were narrowed down to Intermetrics and Cii Honeywell Bull, with the French designers taking the final nod a year later.

Without doubt, the draft version of the proposed standard for Ada, which is here presented, is comprehensive. There are many contributing factors. The requirements set forth by the Department of Defense called for a language with types, subprograms, input-output facilities for numerous devices, as well as parallel processing, exception handling, interfaces to specific hardware, and countless other details. In addition, specific problems, considered paramount by the individuals concerned with the Ada effort, were naturally brought to the fore, as were the concerns of the language design team as a whole. The total of these shared visions has given us a language that is certainly comprehensive.

And so is its power. There is probably no question that the ability of Ada to solve problems is as rich as any programming language.

The first part of this document is an introduction to the Ada programming language. Like any introduction, we emphasize the concepts that form the foundation of the language, rather than attempt to describe the entire language or to provide a self-contained guide for writing programs. Our objective is to convey the essence of the language, mainly through examples.

We assume that the reader has experience in some other higher order programming language. No other particular kind of expertise is assumed.

The introduction is organized in four successive levels:

Chapter 1: This opening chapter provides a very brief sketch of several key features in Ada. The discussion is based on five small example programs.

Chapter 2 through 6: These chapters provide a more thorough treatment of the facilities sketched in Chapter 1. In particular, we treat the concept of data types, the basic statements in the language, subprograms, packages, and general program structure.

Chapter 7 through 11: These chapters describe the facilities needed in many important applications. In particular, we treat some extended concepts in types, input and output facilities, parallel processing, exception handling, and the interface with an implementation.

Chapter 12: Here we present some concluding comments, in conjunction with a full scale example.

A companion document is the language definition itself, the Ada Reference Manual. This document describes the complete language as issued in July 1982 (Military Standard 1815, proposed for Standardization to the American National Standards Institute).

While the Ada effort is obviously the result of many, many persons, four individuals stand out.

William A. Whitaker was primarily responsible for bringing the need for a common computer language to the attention of the Department of Defense, keeping this concern alive during its gestation period, and, in general, nurturing the government support.

David Fisher promoted the effort both inside and outside the Department of Defense, developed the technical requirements, and demonstrated a deep concern for the effort from the very beginning.

William E. Carlson served under DARPA (Defense Advanced Research Projects Agency) as contract officer for the project, took a long-standing interest in the effort, and coordinated the contributions of all participants.

Jean D. Ichbiah, the principal language designer, devoted his immense, and seemingly inexhaustable, energies to the architecture of Ada. While supported by numerous individuals, the final language is, in large part, his own.

As for the introduction to Ada presented here, Andrew Singer provided considerable assistance in its development. Jean Ichbiah gave the project a nihil obstat. Jon Hueras helped design the text formatting program in Chapter 12. Olivier Roubine provided comments, many of them helpful. Bernd Krieg-Brueckner, Philip Wetherall, and Jean-Claude Heliard also contributed to its writing. Michael Marcotty offered his meta-comments; and, finally, Marvin Israel, as editor for Springer-Verlag, provided excellent guidance throughout.

It is, then, with the publication of this volume that we acknowledge the contributions of the Countess and the countless to the development of Ada.

Henry Ledgard
October, 1982

CONTENTS

Specialized Features

Perspective

Chapter 1

FIVE EXAMPLES

Learning to communicate in a new language is always a challenging experience. At first it may seem as though everything is new and all of it must be understood before there is any hope of using the language at all. After a little experience though, it becomes apparent that there are points of reference to our own language. After a while, we realize that both languages have many common roots.

In introducing you to Ada, we take advantage of its similarities to languages in common use, and we urge you as a reader to do the same. In this chapter we present five small programs. These programs provide a sketch of the features in Ada that are common to many other higher order programming languages as well as features that may be novel. In the following five chapters we again sketch these same features, but with much greater detail.

1.1 TEMPERATURE CONVERSION

We write programs in order to interpret and transform data. In writing programs we must describe the nature of the data and give statements for carrying out computations on the data.

Example 1.1 illustrates the structure of a complete program. It has the outline form:

```
with I_O_PACKAGE;
procedure TEMPERATURE_CONVERSION is
    -- a declarative part
    -- describing the data
begin
    -- a statement part
    -- describing the computations
end;
```

Notice how the keywords *procedure*, *is*, *begin*, and *end* form a frame for the program description.

The name of the program is TEMPERATURE_CONVERSION and its form is that of a procedure. A procedure is one form of program unit. The prefix

```
with I_O_PACKAGE;
```

is necessary since the program is using the input-output procedures GET and PUT defined in a library package named I_O_PACKAGE.

The declarative part of our program includes a variable declaration

```
FAHRENHEIT_TEMP, CELSIUS_TEMP: FLOAT;
```

This declaration specifies that the two variables used in the program have the properties of floating point numbers. In general, a declaration associates one or more identifiers with an entity. In this case, the two variable names are objects associated with the type FLOAT. This is characteristic of all programs — every variable must be declared and associated with a given type.

The statement part of our program begins with a subprogram call:

```
GET (FAHRENHEIT_TEMP);
```

This statement calls upon the procedure GET defined in the library package I_O_PACKAGE to obtain a value from some input device and assign the value to the variable FAHRENHEIT_TEMP. The second statement

```
CELSIUS_TEMP := (5.0/9.0) * (FAHRENHEIT_TEMP - 32.0);
```

assigns a newly computed value to the variable CELSIUS_TEMP. The last statement

```
PUT (CELSIUS_TEMP);
```

is like the first and calls upon a subprogram to print the value of the variable CELSIUS_TEMP. Notice that each statement and declaration ends with a semicolon (;).

```
with I_O_PACKAGE;
procedure TEMPERATURE_CONVERSION is
   use I_O_PACKAGE;

   -- A comment.
   -- This program reads a value representing a
   -- fahrenheit temperature and converts it to a
   -- value representing its celsius equivalent.

   FAHRENHEIT_TEMP, CELSIUS_TEMP: FLOAT;

begin

   GET (FAHRENHEIT_TEMP);
   CELSIUS_TEMP := (5.0/9.0) * (FAHRENHEIT_TEMP - 32.0);
   PUT (CELSIUS_TEMP);

end;
```

Example 1.1   Converting temperatures

Our example also contains four lines of comment. All comments begin with -- and are terminated by the end of the line. Comments may generally appear anywhere within a program unit.

Procedures such as GET and PUT which are supplied by a package can be named by dot-notation, for example I_O_PACKAGE.GET and I_O_PACKAGE.PUT. Here we have inserted a use clause

```
use I_O_PACKAGE;
```

at the start of the declarative part, and as a consequence GET and PUT can be named directly.

Finally, an important note. The package I_O_PACKAGE is not part of the standard definition of Ada. This package, used frequently in this introduction, contains many procedures taken from the Ada facility for input and output, and is discussed in Chapter 8.

1.2   COUNTING CHANGE

In many applications we need to store data together. We also need to direct the flow of control in order to perform some computation. These ideas are illustrated in Example 1.2. This program reads in six numbers representing the number of pennies, nickels, dimes, and so forth, given as change, and computes the total value of the change.

```
with I_O_PACKAGE;
procedure COUNT_YOUR_CHANGE is
     use I_O_PACKAGE;

     -- This program reads in 6 integer values, respectively
     -- representing the number of pennies, nickels, dimes, quarters,
     -- half-dollars, and silver dollars in coinage.
     -- The program outputs the total value of the coins in dollars
     -- and cents.

     COIN_COUNT,
     TOTAL_CHANGE,
     NUM_CENTS,
     NUM_DOLLARS: INTEGER;

     COIN_VALUE: constant array (1 .. 6) of INTEGER :=
                 (01, 05, 10, 25, 50, 100);

begin

     TOTAL_CHANGE := 0;
     PUT_LINE ("ENTER THE NUMBER OF EACH COIN");

     for NEXT_COIN in 1 .. 6 loop
        GET (COIN_COUNT);
        TOTAL_CHANGE := TOTAL_CHANGE + COIN_VALUE(NEXT_COIN)*COIN_COUNT;
     end loop;

     NUM_DOLLARS := TOTAL_CHANGE / 100;
     NUM_CENTS   := TOTAL_CHANGE rem 100;

     PUT ("TOTAL CHANGE IS $");  PUT (NUM_DOLLARS);
     if NUM_CENTS < 10 then
        PUT (".0");  PUT (NUM_CENTS);
     else
        PUT (".");   PUT (NUM_CENTS);
     end if;

end;
```

Example 1.2   Counting change

The declarative part of our example program introduces four variables of type INTEGER. The predefined type INTEGER is familiar, and one can perform the conventional operations on integers.

Of more interest to us here is the declaration of an array named COIN_VALUE. The type of COIN_VALUE is specified by the type definition:

```
array (1 .. 6) of INTEGER;
```

Accordingly, COIN_VALUE denotes a collection of six integer components. The components collectively form an array indexed by the subscripts 1 through 6.

The array is initialized with the six integer values:

```
(01, 05, 10, 25, 50, 100)
```

These values respectively represent the value in cents of a penny, nickel, dime, quarter, half dollar, and silver dollar.

The fact that COIN_VALUE is specified as *constant* means that the components of the array must always hold these values, as summarized below:

Array Component	Index	Component Value
COIN_VALUE(1)	1	1
COIN_VALUE(2)	2	5
COIN_VALUE(3)	3	10
COIN_VALUE(4)	4	25
COIN_VALUE(5)	5	50
COIN_VALUE(6)	6	100

The statement part of our program is similar to our previous program, except here we have a *for loop* and an *if statement*. The for loop has the form

```
for NEXT_COIN in 1 .. 6 loop
   -- statements
end loop;
```

The for loop is controlled by the loop parameter NEXT_COIN. The for loop header also specifies that the loop is to be executed for successive values of NEXT_COIN in the range

```
1 .. 6
```

Thus the statements in the loop are executed six times, and upon each iteration NEXT_COIN is assigned one of the values 1 through 6.

The *if* statement has the form

```
if NUM_CENTS < 10 then
   -- statements
else
   -- statements
end if;
```

Here we see the choice of one of two groups of statements based on the value of a condition. If the condition testing the value of NUM_CENTS is true, the first group of statements is executed; otherwise the second group is executed. The choice is made so that, for instance, a dollar and five cents is printed as $1.05, and not as $1.5 where the zero is not printed.

If we examine our program in a little more detail, we can make a few other points. Consider the statement

```
TOTAL_CHANGE := TOTAL_CHANGE + COIN_VALUE(NEXT_COIN)*COIN_COUNT;
```

Here we see the use of the loop parameter NEXT_COIN, which must have one of the values 1 through 6. Notice that the loop parameter is not declared in the declarative part of the program. A loop parameter is implicitly declared by its appearance in a for loop and has the type INTEGER of the values 1 through 6.

Finally, consider the two statements

```
NUM_DOLLARS := TOTAL_CHANGE / 100;
NUM_CENTS    := TOTAL_CHANGE rem 100;
```

Here

```
TOTAL_CHANGE / 100
```

gives the integer part of the quotient resulting from the division of TOTAL_CHANGE by 100, and

```
TOTAL_CHANGE rem 100
```

gives the corresponding integer remainder.

1.3 A BETTER WAY TO COUNT CHANGE

A fundamental aspect in programming is the use of different kinds of objects. Whether the objects are coins, part numbers, tracking positions, or people's names, they must be represented in terms of the constructs of a given programming language.

There are a number of problems with our previous program for counting change. The coins penny through dollar are represented by the integers 1 through 6. Conceptually, coins are simply not numbers. Furthermore, the fact that a dime is represented by 3 even allows us to add a dime to a dime and get 6 (a dollar).

We next revisit our program to count change. Our objective is to illustrate the conceptual unity of declaring *types* as well as to illustrate the greater clarity of types.

The second program for counting change is given in Example 1.3. Its essential differences from the previous example are outlined as follows:

```
procedure COUNT_YOUR_CHANGE is
   ...
   type COIN is (PENNY, NICKEL, DIME, QUARTER, HALF_DOLLAR, DOLLAR);
   ...
   COIN_VALUE: constant array (PENNY .. DOLLAR) of INTEGER :=
               (PENNY  => 01,  NICKEL => 05,      DIME => 10,
                QUARTER => 25, HALF_DOLLAR => 50, DOLLAR => 100);
   ...
begin
   ...
   for NEXT_COIN in PENNY .. DOLLAR loop
      ...
   end loop;
   ...
end;
```

We see here the use of a type named COIN. Unlike the type named INTEGER, the type named COIN is not predefined in the language. It is introduced by the declaration

```
type COIN is (PENNY, NICKEL, DIME, QUARTER, HALF_DOLLAR, DOLLAR);
```

This declaration defines COIN as a type having six values, the identifiers PENNY through DOLLAR. This type is called an *enumeration type.*

The type COIN is used in several places in our program. The first is in the declaration of COIN_VALUE, which has the type definition

```
array (PENNY .. DOLLAR) of INTEGER
```

This definition is analogous to the earlier definition

```
array (1 .. 6) of INTEGER
```

with the important difference that the indices are not denoted by the values 1 through 6 of type INTEGER, but rather by the values PENNY through DOLLAR of type COIN. The components of the array are, of course, integers.

The initialization of the array COIN_VALUE takes advantage of the type COIN in explicitly associating each coin with its corresponding value in cents. In particular, we have

```
(PENNY  => 01,  NICKEL => 05,      DIME => 10,
 QUARTER => 25, HALF_DOLLAR => 50, DOLLAR => 100)
```

```
with I_0_PACKAGE;
procedure COUNT_YOUR_CHANGE is
     use I_0_PACKAGE;

     -- This program reads in 6 integer values, respectively
     -- representing the number of pennies, nickels, dimes, quarters,
     -- half-dollars, and silver dollars in coinage.
     -- The program outputs the total value of the coins in dollars
     -- and cents.

     type COIN is (PENNY, NICKEL, DIME, QUARTER, HALF_DOLLAR, DOLLAR);

     COIN_COUNT,
     TOTAL_CHANGE,
     NUM_CENTS,
     NUM_DOLLARS: INTEGER;

     COIN_VALUE: constant array (PENNY .. DOLLAR) of INTEGER :=
               (PENNY => 01,    NICKEL => 05,       DIME => 10,
                QUARTER => 25, HALF_DOLLAR => 50, DOLLAR => 100);
begin

     TOTAL_CHANGE := 0;
     PUT_LINE ("ENTER THE NUMBER OF EACH COIN");

     for NEXT_COIN in PENNY .. DOLLAR loop
        GET (COIN_COUNT);
        TOTAL_CHANGE := TOTAL_CHANGE + COIN_VALUE(NEXT_COIN)*COIN_COUNT;
     end loop;

     NUM_DOLLARS := TOTAL_CHANGE / 100;
     NUM_CENTS   := TOTAL_CHANGE rem 100;

     PUT ("TOTAL CHANGE IS $");   PUT (NUM_DOLLARS);
     if NUM_CENTS < 10 then
        PUT (".0");   PUT (NUM_CENTS);
     else
        PUT (".");    PUT (NUM_CENTS);
     end if;

end;
```

Example 1.3   Counting change using the type COIN

This listing of index-value pairs is equivalent to the simple listing of the values

    (01, 05, 10, 25, 50, 100)

but takes the guesswork out of interpreting the values. Our COIN_VALUE array may thus be summarized as follows:

Array Component	Index	Component Value
COIN_VALUE(PENNY)	PENNY	1
COIN_VALUE(NICKEL)	NICKEL	5
COIN_VALUE(DIME)	DIME	10
COIN_VALUE(QUARTER)	QUARTER	25
COIN_VALUE(HALF_DOLLAR)	HALF_DOLLAR	50
COIN_VALUE(DOLLAR)	DOLLAR	100

The next use of coin is in the for loop

```
for NEXT_COIN in PENNY .. DOLLAR loop
   -- statements
end loop;
```

Here the values taken on by NEXT_COIN are not the integers in the range

```
1 .. 6
```

but the enumeration values in the range

```
PENNY .. DOLLAR
```

of the type COIN. Thus the loop is still executed six times, but on each iteration NEXT_COIN is successively assigned one of the values PENNY through DOLLAR of type COIN. As before, NEXT_COIN is implicitly declared by its use as the loop parameter, but here NEXT_COIN can only take on values of type COIN and arithmetic may not be performed on these values.

Each of these uses of the type COIN illustrates a general point. The type COIN represents a conceptual unit introduced by the programmer. Rather than rely on representing coins as integers, the programmer can capture the notion of a coin by giving it a type definition of its own. The use of this type has the added security that once a variable has a coin type, it can only take on values of this type.

1.4 TARGET PRACTICE

The ability to organize programs into subprograms is an important part of every programming language. Furthermore, the ability to parameterize a subprogram allows a programmer to summarize its behavior in terms of its logical inputs and outputs.

These ideas are illustrated in the program of Example 1.4. This program reads in the initial X and Y velocities of a projectile, as well as the distance to a target on the same level and the height of the target. The program determines whether the projectile will hit the target using simple laws of physics.

```
with I_O_PACKAGE;
procedure TARGET_PRACTICE is
   use I_O_PACKAGE;

   -- This program reads in four values, respectively representing
   -- the initial X and Y velocities of a projectile, the distance
   -- to a target, and the height of the target.
   -- It prints a message indicating whether the projectile will
   -- hit the target or not.

   G: constant FLOAT := 9.81; -- meters per second per second

   X_VELOCITY, Y_VELOCITY,
   TARGET_DISTANCE, TARGET_HEIGHT, NET_RISE: FLOAT;

   procedure COMPUTE_RISE (V_X, V_Y, DISTANCE: in FLOAT;
                           RISE: out FLOAT) is
      TIME: FLOAT;
   begin
      TIME := DISTANCE / V_X;
      RISE := V_Y*TIME - (G/2.0)*(TIME**2);
   end;

begin

   PUT_LINE ("ENTER X AND Y VELOCITIES, DISTANCE, AND HEIGHT:");
   GET (X_VELOCITY);
   GET (Y_VELOCITY);
   GET (TARGET_DISTANCE);
   GET (TARGET_HEIGHT);

   COMPUTE_RISE (X_VELOCITY, Y_VELOCITY, TARGET_DISTANCE, NET_RISE);

   if NET_RISE > 0.0 and NET_RISE < TARGET_HEIGHT then
      PUT ("HIT");
   else
      PUT ("MISS");
   end if;

end;
```

Example 1.4 Target practice

Our interest in this example centers on the subprogram COMPUTE_RISE, which has the following outline:

```
procedure COMPUTE_RISE (V_X, V_Y, DISTANCE: in FLOAT;
                        RISE: out FLOAT) is
   -- local declarations
begin
   -- local statements
end;
```

This subprogram has three input parameters and one output parameter, each of type FLOAT. Inside the subprogram, the parameters have the names V_X, V_Y, DISTANCE, and RISE. These parameters characterize the behavior of the subprogram. Internally, the subprogram computes a value for RISE based on the three inputs V_X, V_Y, and DISTANCE.

This subprogram is used in the main program, which contains the subprogram call:

```
COMPUTE_RISE (X_VELOCITY, Y_VELOCITY, TARGET_DISTANCE, NET_RISE);
```

Corresponding to the definition of the subprogram COMPUTE_RISE, the subprogram call contains four arguments, each of type FLOAT. The first three arguments give the three input values for the procedure. After the call, the fourth argument NET_RISE will take on the output value computed for the parameter RISE.

Our example also illustrates another basic idea. Program units (in this case procedure subprograms) can be nested. In our case we have the structure:

```
procedure TARGET_PRACTICE is
    . . .
    procedure COMPUTE_RISE (parameters) is
        . . .
    end;
    . . .
end;
```

Notice that the inner program unit COMPUTE_RISE refers to the acceleration due to gravity constant G that is declared in the outer unit. Notice also that the inner unit contains the declaration of a local variable TIME. Thus we see the dual role of nesting. An inner unit may refer to global information given in an outer unit, and it may also contain information that is (and should be) entirely internal.

1.5 KEEPING SCORE

A central feature of Ada is the ability to collect data, types, and subprograms into a unit that can be used in other programs. This feature is, naturally enough, called a *package*.

Consider the simple package shown in Example 1.5a. Here five data types, two constants, and a procedure are defined, each relevant to the given application. In particular, the declaration

```
type HOLE_NUMBER is range 1 .. 18;
```

defines a numeric type whose values are the integers in the range 1 through 18.

```
package GOLF_INFO is

    type GOLF_CLUB   is (DRIVER, IRON, PUTTER, WEDGE, MASHIE);
    type GOLF_SCORE  is range 1 .. 200;
    type HOLE_NUMBER is range 1 .. 18;
    type HANDICAP    is range 0 .. 36;
    type SCORE_DATA  is array (HOLE_NUMBER) of GOLF_SCORE;

    PAR_FOR_COURSE: constant GOLF_SCORE := 72;
    PAR_VALUES:  constant SCORE_DATA :=
                (1 => 5,  2 => 3,  3 => 4,  4 => 4,  5 => 3,  6 => 4,
                 7 => 5,  8 => 4,  9 => 4, 10 => 3, 11 => 4, 12 => 4,
                13 => 4, 14 => 5, 15 => 3, 16 => 4, 17 => 4, 18 => 5);

    procedure COMPUTE_TOTAL (SCORES: in SCORE_DATA;
                             TOTAL : out GOLF_SCORE);
end;


package body GOLF_INFO is

    procedure COMPUTE_TOTAL (SCORES: in SCORE_DATA;
                             TOTAL : out GOLF_SCORE) is
    begin
      TOTAL := 0;
      for HOLE in HOLE_NUMBER loop
         TOTAL := TOTAL + SCORES(HOLE);
      end loop;
    end;

end;
```

Example 1.5a   A golf package

Notice also the procedure header:

```
procedure COMPUTE_TOTAL (SCORES: in SCORE_DATA;
                         TOTAL : out GOLF_SCORE);
```

Like the declaration of the type HOLE_NUMBER or the declaration of the constant PAR_FOR_COURSE, the procedure header is a *declaration* of a procedure named COMPUTE_TOTAL.

All of these declared items are collected together in the form:

```
package GOLF_INFO is
    -- declarations
end;
```

These declarations are called the *visible part* of the package.

```
with GOLF_INFO, I_O_PACKAGE;
procedure KEEP_SCORE is
    use GOLF_INFO, I_O_PACKAGE;

    -- This program reads in the golf scores for each of 18 holes.
    -- It computes the total score and the amount over (or under) par.

    MY_SCORES  :  SCORE_DATA;
    TOTAL_SCORE:  GOLF_SCORE;

begin
    PUT ("LET'S HAVE THE SCORES FOR EACH HOLE.");
    for HOLE in HOLE_NUMBER loop
        NEW_LINE;
        PUT (HOLE); PUT (" = ");
        GET (MY_SCORES(HOLE));
    end loop;

    COMPUTE_TOTAL (MY_SCORES, TOTAL_SCORE);
    NEW_LINE;
    PUT ("YOUR TOTAL IS ");  PUT (TOTAL_SCORE);

    NEW_LINE;
    if TOTAL_SCORE < PAR_FOR_COURSE then
        PUT (PAR_FOR_COURSE - TOTAL_SCORE);  PUT ( " UNDER PAR." );
    elsif TOTAL_SCORE = PAR_FOR_COURSE then
        PUT ("AN EVEN PAR");
    else
        PUT (TOTAL_SCORE - PAR_FOR_COURSE);  PUT (" OVER PAR.");
    end if;
end;
```

Example 1.5b Using the golf package

To complete the definition of the package, the computations performed by the procedure COMPUTE_TOTAL must be defined. This is accomplished with a *package body*, which has the form:

```
package body GOLF_INFO is
    -- definition of procedure COMPUTE_TOTAL
end;
```

Here, the complete procedure is defined. Both the visible part of the package as well as the package body can be separately compiled.

The package GOLF_INFO can be used in another program unit, as illustrated in Example 1.5b. This program unit has the form

```
with GOLF_INFO, I_O_PACKAGE;
procedure KEEP_SCORE is
    -- local declarations
begin
    -- statements
end;
```

and makes use of some of the items specified in the visible part of the package GOLF_INFO. Notice, for example, the declaration

```
MY_SCORES: SCORE_DATA;
```

which introduces an array names MY_SCORES whose type, SCORE_DATA, is declared in the visible part of the package. Notice also the call

```
COMPUTE_TOTAL (MY_SCORES, TOTAL_SCORE);
```

to the procedure COMPUTE_TOTAL declared in the visible part of the package.

Example 1.5 brings up a number of general points about the use of packages. First, a package is generally defined in two parts: the visible part, which specifies the items that may be made available to other program units, and the package body, which completes the definition of the items in the visible part. The package body is omitted if the visible part is self-contained.

Second, a package can be separately compiled. Any other program unit that uses the package must name the package in a with clause at the beginning of the program unit.

Third, a use clause of the form

```
use package-name;
```

makes the items in the visible part directly available in the program unit containing the use clause.

Packages are a somewhat novel feature of Ada, and will be treated in more detail later. Nevertheless, they are an important program development tool. They allow groups of related information to be collected together and made available to users on a selective basis. Like subprograms, only their public interface is exposed to the user.

Chapter 2

DESCRIBING DATA

In every application we have many kinds of objects, each with different properties. To solve a problem properly, we must describe real world objects and their properties in terms of the constructs of a given programming language. Moreover, we must not only choose an appropriate description for an entity, but must make sure that an operation validly performed in a program has a meaning in terms of the real world objects and operations.

For instance, we can perform the conventional arithmetic operation on numeric data, but while we can describe calendar dates as integers and can subtract two dates to get an interval of time, it does not make any sense to take the square root of a date or to multiply a date by a velocity.

We thus see two critical programming issues:

■ The need to describe objects and their properties with precision and clarity.

■ The need to guarantee that the operations over objects do not violate their intrinsic properties.

This leads us to the concept of types.

2.1   TYPES

We begin with two examples:

```
type DAY  is (MON, TUE, WED, THU, FRI, SAT, SUN);
type COIN is (PENNY, NICKEL, DIME, QUARTER, HALF_DOLLAR, DOLLAR);
```

The first declaration introduces a type named DAY, the second a type named COIN. Just as we can say

```
COUNTER: INTEGER;
```

to declare a variable COUNTER of type INTEGER, we can say

```
TODAY: DAY;
```

to declare a variable TODAY of type DAY. Similarly, just as a variable of type INTEGER can take on integer values, a variable of type DAY can take on one of the seven values MON through SUN. It is in this sense that we say a type describes a class of values.

The two types introduced above are called *enumeration types*. For enumeration types, the type declaration explicitly enumerates the class of values.

One of the properties of every enumeration type is that the values are ordered. In particular, the values are assumed to be enumerated in increasing order. For the type DAY, the first value is MON, the last is SUN.

For every type there are operations that can validly be performed on the values. For enumeration types, these include the relational operators for comparing values in the type. Thus if the variable TODAY has the value TUE, we may have the following expressions:

```
TODAY  = MON    -- test for equality, value is FALSE
TODAY <= FRI    -- test for less than or equal, value is TRUE
```

The above examples illustrate a basic idea: a programmer can introduce a type to describe a class of values needed for an application.

Programmer defined types are introduced by type declarations of the form:

```
type identifier is type-definition;
```

The identifier specifies a name for the type. The type definition specifies the class of values and implicitly, the operations defining ways in which the values can be used. Importantly, every type definition introduces a distinct type.

With this discussion in mind, we give the basic definition of a type:

■   A type characterizes a set of values and the set of operations that are applicable to the values.

In programs, all variables have an associated type. The type is that specified when the variable is declared.

One of the key issues in programming is the security with which we can draw conclusions about a program. Consider the following declarations:

```
TODAY    : DAY;
NEW_COIN : COIN;
COUNTER  : INTEGER;
```

It would be meaningful to have the statements

```
TODAY    := TUE;
NEW_COIN := NICKEL;
COUNTER  := COUNTER + 1;
```

but not meaningful to have the statements

```
TODAY    := NICKEL;    -- NICKEL is not a day
NEW_COIN := TUE;       -- TUE is not a coin
COUNTER  := TODAY + 1; -- addition is not a legal operation for days
```

This leads us to the two basic rules for using types:

1. A variable cannot be assigned a value of a different type.

2. The only allowed operations on a value are those associated with the definition of its type.

These rules are strictly enforced by the language compiler, and any type errors are reported during compilation. We can thus draw a fundamental conclusion guaranteed by the use of types.

■   The type properties declared by a programmer will not be violated during program execution.

Once the type of a variable has been declared, the programmer can refer to some of the properties of the type using the notation for predefined attributes. A predefined attribute has the form:

entity'attribute-designator

Returning to enumeration types, we can refer to the first and last values of the type DAY with the attributes:

```
DAY'FIRST  -- the first value of the type DAY
DAY'LAST   -- the last value of the type DAY
```

In addition, the functions for computing next and previous values of the enumeration type DAY can be denoted by the function attributes SUCC (for successor) and PRED (for predecessor):

```
DAY'SUCC(TUE) = WED
DAY'PRED(TUE) = MON
```

Taking the successor of SUN or the predecessor of MON gives an error, which unfortunately is not quite right for working with the days of the week.

As mentioned earlier, an enumeration type is defined by enumerating its values. Such types can be used as freely as integers, and often with great clarity. For example, we may declare a table itemizing the number of hours worked on each day of the week

```
HOURS_WORKED: array (MON .. SUN) of INTEGER;
```

or equivalently

```
HOURS_WORKED: array (DAY'FIRST .. DAY'LAST) of INTEGER;
```

or even:

```
HOURS_WORKED: array (DAY) of INTEGER;
```

Further, we have a loop iterating over the days of the week

```
for CURRENT_DAY in MON .. SUN loop
   -- what to do for each value of CURRENT_DAY
end loop;
```

or equivalently:

```
for CURRENT_DAY in DAY'FIRST .. DAY'LAST loop
   -- what to do for each value of CURRENT_DAY
end loop;
```

Notice the clarity of the above loops over:

```
for DAY_INDEX in 1 .. 7 loop
   -- what to do for each value of DAY_INDEX
end loop;
```

Table 2.1 defines a number of enumeration types. Using such types can add considerably to the expressiveness of a program.

Table 2.1
A Sampler of Enumeration Types

```
type DAY         is   (MON, TUE, WED, THU, FRI, SAT, SUN);

type COIN        is   (PENNY, NICKEL, DIME, QUARTER, HALF_DOLLAR, DOLLAR);

type DIRECTION   is   (NORTH, EAST, SOUTH, WEST);

type OP_CODE     is   (ADD, SUB, MUL, LDA, STA, STZ);

type HALF_DAY    is   (AM, PM);

type FILE_STATUS is   (OPEN, CLOSED);

type ARMY_RANK   is   (PRIVATE, CORPORAL, SERGEANT, LIEUTENANT,
                       CAPTAIN, MAJOR, COLONEL, GENERAL);

type CONTROL_CHAR is  (NULL, END_OF_TRANSMISSION, ENQUIRE, BELL,
                       BACKSPACE, LINE_FEED, CANCEL, ESCAPE);

type PEN_STATUS  is   (DOWN, UP);

type SHAPE       is   (TRIANGLE, QUADRANGLE, PENTAGON, HEXAGON);

type DRIVING_CODE is  (NORMAL, LIMITED, SPECIAL, VIP);

type LETTER      is   ('A', 'B', 'C', 'D', 'E', 'F', 'G', 'H', 'I',
                       'J', 'K', 'L', 'M', 'N', 'O', 'P', 'Q', 'R',
                       'S', 'T', 'U', 'V', 'W', 'X', 'Y', 'Z');

type HEX_LETTER  is   ('A', 'B', 'C', 'D', 'E', 'F');
```

2.2 PRIMITIVE TYPES

In any language there are several types that are so commonly used that they are defined in the language itself. These are the primitive types. These basic types are not only useful in their own right, but can be used to define other, more elaborate, types needed in an application.

Perhaps the simplest of all primitive types is the type named BOOLEAN. This type captures the idea of truth and falsity. It is in fact a predefined enumeration type with two values, FALSE and TRUE.

In addition to the properties common to all enumeration types, several logical operations are defined for boolean values. These include the operators

```
and   -- logical conjunction, e.g. (TRUE and FALSE) = FALSE
or    -- logical disjunction, e.g. (TRUE or FALSE) = TRUE
not   -- logical negation,    e.g. (not TRUE) = FALSE
```

Another important predefined type is the enumeration type named CHARACTER. Characters are used to form messages and text. The allowed characters and their ordering are those defined for the ASCII character set. Single character literals are enclosed by single quotes. You have to be a bit careful here, as *strings* of characters are enclosed by double quotes. Thus we have:

```
'A'   -- the character A
"A"   -- the string A of length one
```

No language would be very useful without some facility for arithmetic computation. The most familiar arithmetic type is the type named INTEGER used for exact arithmetic. This type denotes a finite subset of the whole numbers. The range of integer values is implicitly limited by the representation adopted by a given implementation. The operations over this type are familiar, and includes the arithmetic operators

```
+   -- addition
-   -- subtraction
*   -- multiplication
/   -- division
```

as well as the relational operators

```
<    -- less than
<=   -- less than or equal to
=    -- equal
/=   -- not equal
>=   -- greater than or equal to
>    -- greater than
```

The relational operators all yield a result of type BOOLEAN.

The arithmetic types also include the real types. Real types provide approximations to the real numbers. With a fixed point real type, the accuracy of the type is specified by giving an absolute error bound. With a floating point real type, the accuracy of the type is specified by giving a relative error bound. Consider the following declarations:

```
type VOLTAGE is delta 0.1 range 0.0 .. 10.0; -- a fixed point type
type WEIGHT  is digits 10;                    -- a floating point type
```

The type VOLTAGE denotes a set of fixed point numbers whose values have an accuracy at least as fine as 0.1. The type WEIGHT denotes a set of floating point numbers whose values have an accuracy of at least 10 digits. As for integers, the arithmetic and relational operators are defined for real types.

A given implementation may have one or more predefined real types, for example, the types named FLOAT, LONG_FLOAT, and so forth. These types would be likely to correspond to the arithmetic supplied by the hardware.

One somewhat pleasant feature of Ada is that numbers can be written with medial underscores. Thus for example, the numbers

```
1000000
022325795
```

which may denote an amount of money and a social security number, respectively, may also be written as:

```
1_000_000
022_32_5795
```

Before leaving the primitive types, we emphasize two fundamental points. The types BOOLEAN and CHARACTER, as well as the arithmetic types and programmer defined enumeration types, each represent a conceptual unit for describing a class of values. Furthermore, the type properties declared by the programmer remain invariant during program execution. This ensures, for example, that an integer variable always denotes an integer, and that we cannot inadvertently add a character to a real number or compare a day of the week to an integer.

2.3 ARRAY TYPES

We must have ways to represent objects like a directory of area codes, a deck of cards, or a line of characters. These objects are different from those described earlier in this section in that their structure is of interest. In particular, they have components that bear some relation to each other.

Perhaps the most familiar of such objects in programming are arrays. An *array* is a collection of components of the same component type. In its simplest form an array is a description of a table. Consider the following table, which describes the number of hours worked on each day of the week:

Day	Hours Worked
Monday	8
Tuesday	8
Wednesday	8
Thursday	10
Friday	8
Saturday	0
Sunday	0

Given the enumeration type DAY declared above, this table could be declared as:

```
HOURS_WORKED: array (DAY'FIRST .. DAY'LAST) of INTEGER;
```

Just as for enumeration types, array type definitions can be named in a type declaration and the name can be used to declare array variables. For example, we may have:

```
type WORK_DATA is array (DAY'FIRST .. DAY'LAST) of INTEGER;
HOURS_WORKED: WORK_DATA;
```

An intrinsic property of each array is that it has indices. The allowable indices are specified by giving a range of discrete values. For example, we may have the array type definitions:

```
array (DAY'FIRST .. DAY'LAST) of INTEGER
array (MON .. SUN) of INTEGER
array (DAY) of INTEGER
```

Each of these definitions is equivalent. The indices are the values MON through SUN of type DAY. For any array A, the lower bound of its first index is denoted with the attribute A'FIRST, the upper bound with A'LAST.

A basic operation on arrays is indexing. It permits referencing and updating of components. For example, with the declarations

```
I: INTEGER;
A: array (1 .. 10) of INTEGER;

TODAY        : DAY;
HOURS_WORKED: array (DAY'FIRST .. DAY'LAST) of INTEGER;
```

and the assignments

```
I     := 1;
TODAY := MON;
```

we may update the first components of A and HOURS_WORKED with

```
A(I) := A(I) + 1;
HOURS_WORKED(TODAY) := HOURS_WORKED(TODAY) + 1;
```

In addition to indexing, assignment and equality are defined on complete arrays. The value of a complete array can be denoted by the array name. It can also be constructed by giving an aggregate. An *aggregate* is a listing of the values of each component. These values can be given in positional order, or by giving each component index and its associated value.

For example, each one of the following assignments would set the value of
HOURS_WORKED to the values given in the previous table:

```
HOURS_WORKED := (8, 8, 8, 10, 8, 0, 0);

HOURS_WORKED := (MON => 8, TUE => 8, WED => 8, THU =>10,
                 FRI => 8, SAT => 0, SUN => 0);

HOURS_WORKED := (MON | TUE | WED | FRI => 8,  THU => 10,
                 SAT | SUN => 0;
```

Notice that when the indices are explicitly given, the component values can be
listed in any order. Notice also that array assignment requires that the number
of components assigned be identical to the number declared for the array
variable.

The notation for aggregates has several other forms that are especially
useful for large arrays. For example, for an array

```
B: array (1 .. 100) of INTEGER;
```

the aggregate

```
(1..100 => 0)
```

denotes an array value where all components are zero. If the first four
components are one, and the remaining components are zero, we may use the
aggregate

```
(1 => 1,  2 => 1,  3 => 1,  4 => 1,  5..100 => 0)
```

or

```
(1..4 => 1,  5..100 => 0)
```

or even:

```
(1..4 => 1,  others => 0)
```

Here the choice *others* stands for all remaining values.

In addition to operating on complete arrays, portions of an array can be
denoted by an array slice. An array *slice* is a consecutive sequence of
components of a one-dimensional array. For example, the first ten components
of the array B above can be denoted by the slice:

```
B(1 .. 10)
```

These ten components can be assigned the values of the last ten components
with the assignment:

```
B(1..10)  :=  B(91..100);
```

Arrays With Unspecified Index Ranges

Consider the problem of writing a procedure to compute the maximum value in any array with integer components, no matter how many components are in the array. This problem is typical of cases where we want to define an array operation for which the range of the indices is unspecified.

The problem of dealing with arrays of arbitrary size can be handled by giving the type of the indices but leaving the range of the indices unspecified. Such an array is called an *unconstrained* array. Variables of such a type must, in turn, be declared with a specific index range.

Consider, for example, the following declarations:

```
NUM_APPLICANTS: constant INTEGER := 20;
NUM_EMPLOYEES : constant INTEGER := 1000;

MAX_SCORE, MAX_WAGE: INTEGER;

type ANY_INTEGER_ARRAY is array (INTEGER range <>) of INTEGER;

SCORE_TABLE: ANY_INTEGER_ARRAY(1 .. NUM_APPLICANTS);
WAGE_TABLE : ANY_INTEGER_ARRAY(1 .. NUM_EMPLOYEES);
```

Here, the type ANY_INTEGER_ARRAY defines a class of arrays with integer components and integer indices. The symbol <> (a < followed by a >) is used to indicate the possible *range* for an index that is unspecified. The variables SCORE_TABLE and WAGE_TABLE both are of this type, but with a specifically given index range.

We can now readily write a procedure for calculating the maximum value of an array of arbitrary size:

```
procedure GET_MAX (A: in ANY_INTEGER_ARRAY;  MAX: out INTEGER) is
begin
   MAX := A(A'FIRST);
   for I in (A'FIRST + 1) .. A'LAST loop
     if A(I) > MAX then
        MAX := A(I);
     end if;
   end loop;
end;
```

Notice here that the attributes A'FIRST and A'LAST allow us to make use of the actual bounds of a given array argument. This procedure can thus be applied to our two arrays with the calls:

```
GET_MAX (SCORE_TABLE, MAX_SCORE);
GET_MAX (WAGE_TABLE, MAX_WAGE);
```

Strings

Strings are the basic units for describing messages and text, and thus have an important role in many applications, especially those with extensive input and output. The predefined type named STRING is a predefined array type with character components and integer indices. The range of the indices is unspecified, but the lower bound must be 1 or greater.

Since STRING is an array type, a variable of type STRING can be declared by giving the bounds of its indices. For example, we can say:

```
FIRST_NAME, LAST_NAME: STRING(1 .. 10);
INPUT_LINE: STRING(1 .. 72)
```

Explicit character strings can be written in the familiar way, by enclosing the sequence of characters within double quotes. For example, we can write:

```
FIRST_NAME := "GEORGE    ";
LAST_NAME  := "WASHINGTON";

PUT ("THIS MESSAGE");
```

Observe that an explicit character string can be viewed as a shorthand notation for a positional array aggregate. The number of components in the aggregate is the number of characters in the string.

Watch out though for one major snag. Since strings are represented as arrays, a string value must have the same number of characters as a string variable to which it is assigned. Thus, much as you would like, you cannot say:

```
FIRST_NAME := "GEORGE";    -- trouble, 10 characters needed
```

There are ways to reduce this problem, for example using procedures with unconstrained arrays as parameters as in GET_MAX above, but you must be careful.

Finally, the concatenation operator & can be applied to strings. For example, we can write:

```
INPUT_LINE(1..20) := FIRST_NAME & LAST_NAME;
```

This completes our first look at types in Ada. There is more to come, and we shall continue in Chapter 7.

Chapter 3

DESCRIBING
COMPUTATIONS

Every language includes constructs for calculating values, making decisions, and computing results. We turn next to these constructs, the basic expressions and statements in the language. These constructs are familiar to all programmers, but in Ada you will find them especially well-designed.

3.1 EXPRESSIONS

An expression is a formula for computing a value. The basic elements of an expression are typified by the following examples:

```
2                   -- a numeric value
TRUE                -- a boolean value
MON                 -- an enumeration value
"ILLEGAL SYMBOL"    -- a string value
(1 .. 10 => 0)      -- an aggregate value

INDEX               -- the value of a variable
TEXT(I + 1)         -- the value of an array component

A(1 .. 10)          -- a slice of an array
LENGTH(TOKEN)       -- the value of a function call
A'FIRST             -- the value of an attribute
```

The elements of an expression can be combined with operators. As is customary, we can use parentheses to specify the order of evaluation, or in the absence of parentheses, there are precedence levels specifying the order of evaluation. For instance, the multiplying operations * and / are applied before the adding operators + and –, the adding operators are applied before the relational operators = and < and the relational operators are applied before the logical operators *and* and *or*.

In order to maintain the security afforded by types, each operator in an expression is applicable only to operands of specified types, and yields a result of some specified type. For example, the adding operators + and – are only applicable to numeric values of the same type and yield a result of the same type.

For instance, with the declarations

```
type DOLLAR_AMOUNT  is range -10000 .. +10000;
type HOLE_NUMBER    is range 1 .. 18;

SALARY, BONUS: DOLLAR_AMOUNT;
NEXT_HOLE    : HOLE_NUMBER:
```

the following expressions are valid

```
SALARY - 100     -- result is of type DOLLAR_AMOUNT
SALARY + BONUS   -- result is of type DOLLAR_AMOUNT
NEXT_HOLE + 1    -- result is of type HOLE_NUMBER
```

whereas

```
SALARY + 100.0      -- 100.0 is not of type DOLLAR_AMOUNT
SALARY + NEXT_HOLE  -- different named types
```

are not.

A summary of some of the operators in Ada and the type rules for their valid use are given in Table 3.1. These operators may be combined in traditional ways, as in the following expressions:

```
LINE_POS + SYMBOL_LENGTH  -- simple addition
LINE_COUNT mod PAGE_SIZE  -- remainder after modulo integer division
not SYMBOL_FOUND          -- logical negation
SQRT(B**2 - 4.0*A*C)      -- computation of a real value

I in 1 .. 10              -- range test for I

INDEX < LINE_SIZE         -- boolean valued test
WARM or (COLD and SUNNY)  -- boolean valued test
```

Table 3.1
Some Basic Operations

Unary operators:

Operator	Operation	Operand Type	Result Type
+	identity	numeric	same numeric type
–	negation	numeric	same numeric type
abs	absolute value	numeric	numeric
not	logical negation	boolean	boolean

Binary operators for operands of identical type:

Operator	Operation	Operand Type	Result Type
+	addition	numeric	same numeric type
–	subtraction	numeric	same numeric type
mod	modulus	integer	same integer type
rem	remainder	integer	same integer type
= /=	equality and inequality	any type	BOOLEAN
< <= > >=	test for ordering	any scalar type	BOOLEAN
and	conjunction	boolean	BOOLEAN
or	inclusive disjunction	boolean	BOOLEAN

Binary operators for operands of differing type:

Operator	Operation	Left Operand	Right Operand	Result Type
*	multiplication	integer	integer	same integer type
		floating	floating	same floating type
		fixed	INTEGER	same as Left
		INTEGER	fixed	same as Right
		fixed	fixed	universal-fixed
/	division	integer	integer	same integer type
		floating	floating	same floating type
		fixed	integer	same as Left
		fixed	fixed	universal-fixed
**	exponentiation	integer	integer	same as left
		floating	integer	same as left
in not in	membership	any type T	range or subtype of T	BOOLEAN

3.2 ASSIGNMENT STATEMENTS

A fundamental operation in almost every programming language is assignment, whereby the current value of a variable is replaced by a new value specified by an expression. An assignment statement has the form:

variable := expression;

The variable and the expression can be of any type, including for example complete arrays and array slices. However, as we recall from our discussion on types, the variable and expression must have the same type. This rule guarantees that the type properties of variables are preserved during program execution.

For example, consider the following assignments:

```
INDEX      := 0;                -- a simple initialization
TODAY      := TUE;              -- assignment of a day
DISCRIM    := (B**2 - 4.0*A*C); -- assignment of a real value

SYMBOL_FOUND  := FALSE;         -- a boolean initialization
SYMBOL_LENGTH := SIZE(TOKEN);   -- assignment of a function result
TABLE(J)      := TABLE(I) + 1;  -- a table update

TEXT(1 .. 4)  := "JOHN";        -- assignment of a string value
VECTOR        := (1 .. 10 => 0); -- setting of an array to zero
```

Given appropriate declarations, all of these assignments are valid. Notice that with the use of suitable types, the values assigned can well reflect the real world objects they are intended to represent.

Finally, we recall that any constraints on a variable are checked upon assignment. This guarantees that any attempted violation, for example assigning a negative value to NEXT_HOLE, will be reported to the programmer.

3.3 CONDITIONAL STATEMENTS

Different situations demand different computations. The notion of conditional selection is handled by two statements, the *if* statement and the *case* statement.

The if statement allows the selection of a sequence of statements based on the truth value of one or more conditions. For example, we may have a single condition, as in:

```
if (MONTH_NAME = DEC) and (DAY_NUM = 31) then
   MONTH_NAME := JAN;
   DAY_NUM    := 1;
   YEAR_NUM   := YEAR_NUM + 1;
end if;
```

Here the truth or falsity of the condition

```
(MONTH_NAME = DEC) and (DAY_NUM = 31)
```

determines whether or not the enclosed sequence of statements is executed. Note that the parentheses are not actually needed in this condition and have only been put in for clarity.

With multiple conditions it is the first true condition that determines which sequence of statements is executed. For example, we may have a structure like:

```
if WEATHER_CONDITION = RAIN then
    -- sequence of statements describing
    -- what to do when it rains
elsif WEATHER_CONDITION = SUNSHINE then
    -- sequence of statements describing
    -- what to do when the sun shines
else
    -- sequence of statements describing
    -- what to do if it is not raining
    -- and the sun is not shining
end if;
```

More generally, a condition is any expression whose type is BOOLEAN. Thus the selecting conditions can be quite varied, as in:

```
if SYMBOL_FOUND then ...          -- use of a boolean variable
if INDEX < LINE_SIZE then ...     -- use of a relation
if X in 1 .. 100 then ...         -- test for range membership
if A(1 .. 10) = A(11 .. 20) then ...  -- comparison of array slices
if OCCUPIED(ROW, COL) then ...    -- a boolean function call
```

A case statement is analogous to an if statement except that the selection is based on the value of a single expression given at the head of the case statement. For example, consider the case statement:

```
case TODAY is
    when MON => OPEN_ACCOUNTS;
                COMPUTE_INITIAL_BALANCE;
    when TUE => GENERATE_REPORT (TODAY);
    when WED => GENERATE_REPORT (TODAY);
    when THU => GENERATE_REPORT (TODAY);
    when FRI => COMPUTE_CLOSING_BALANCE;
                CLOSE_ACCOUNTS;
    when SAT => null;
    when SUN => null;
end case;
```

Based on the value of TODAY of type DAY, one of the seven case alternatives will be selected. Here, as in all case statements, an alternative must be provided for each possible value of the selecting expression.

The selection values given in a when clause are not limited to single values. In particular, a listing of values or a range of values may be given. Thus the case statement above could also be written:

```
case TODAY is
    when MON        => OPEN_ACCOUNTS;
                       COMPUTE_INITIAL BALANCE;
    when TUE..THU   => GENERATE_REPORT(TODAY);
    when FRI        => COMPUTE_CLOSING_BALANCE;
                       CLOSE_ACCOUNTS;
    when SAT | SUN  => null;
end case;
```

Finally, there are instances where the selecting expression has multiple values and where, except for a few values, the actions to be taken are identical. In these instances the choice *others* may be used to cover any values not given in the previous choices. For example we may have

```
case TODAY is
    when MON     => INITIALIZE_PAY_DATA;
    when FRI     => WRITE_PAYCHECKS;
    when others  => null;
end case;
```

The choice *others* must always appear last.

3.4 LOOPING STATEMENTS

The basic mechanism for repeated calculations is the *loop statement*. The repeated calculations form the basic loop and are always bracketed in the form:

```
loop
    -- statements to be repeated
end loop;
```

A basic loop can be prefixed by an iteration clause or contain loop exit statements within the basic loop. Execution of the basic loop terminates when the iteration clause is completed or when a loop exit statement is executed.

One form of iteration clause is a *for clause*, which defines a loop parameter and a range of values that are successively assigned to the parameter on each iteration. For example, we may have the loop:

```
SUM := 0;
for I in 1 .. 10 loop
   SUM := SUM + A(I);
end loop;
```

This loop sums ten elements of the array A.

More generally, the loop parameter can be of any discrete type whose range of values is given explicitly. For example we may have

```
for DAY in MON .. FRI loop
   -- statements to be executed for successive values of
   -- DAY from MON through FRI
end loop;
```

or:

```
for NEXT_COIN in COIN'FIRST .. COIN'LAST loop
   -- statements to be executed for successive values of
   -- NEXT_COIN from COIN'FIRST through COIN'LAST
end loop;
```

The range of values may also be given by naming a discrete type, as in:

```
for NEXT_COIN in COIN loop
   -- statements to be executed for successive values of
   -- NEXT_COIN from COIN'FIRST to COIN'LAST
end loop;
```

The second form of iteration specification is a *while clause*, which defines a condition that is tested before each execution of the basic loop. The loop is terminated when the while clause evaluates to false. For example, we may have the loops:

```
while NEXT_CHAR /= TERMINATOR loop
   SKIP_CHAR (FILE_NAME, NEXT_CHAR);
end loop;

while X > EPSILON loop
   X := F(X, Y);
   Y := G(X, Y);
end loop;
```

As mentioned above, loops may also contain explicit exit statements. For example, consider the loop:

```
loop
    GET_COMMAND (DEVICE, COMMAND);
    exit when (COMMAND_STATUS = STOP);
    PROCESS_COMMAND (USER, COMMAND);
end loop;
```

This loop continues to get and process commands until the status of the input command designates a stop.

Finally, loops can be labeled, and an exit statement within the loop can be used to cause termination of the labeled loop. For example, we may have:

```
FIND:
    for I in 1 .. 10 loop
        for J in 1 .. 20 loop
            if A(I, J) = 0 then
                M := I;
                N := J;
                exit FIND;
            end if;
        end loop;
    end loop FIND;
```

Here both loops are terminated when a zero-valued array component is found.

Chapter 4

SUBPROGRAMS

We are all familiar with the concept of a subprogram and could hardly imagine a programming language without some such feature. Subprograms allow the programmer to package (often elaborate) computations and parameterize their behavior.

4.1 SUBPROGRAMS

In Ada, there are two forms of subprograms — *procedures* and *functions*. Procedure subprograms allow the definition of a sequence of actions; procedures are invoked with a subprogram call statement. Function subprograms allow the definition of a computation returning a value; functions are invoked with a function call within an expression. Side-effects, that is assignments to global variables, are allowed within both functions and procedures.

Consider the following subprogram, given earlier in Section 1.4:

```
procedure COMPUTE_RISE(V_X, V_Y, DISTANCE: in FLOAT;
                       RISE: out FLOAT) is
   TIME : FLOAT;
begin
   TIME := DISTANCE / V_X;
   RISE := V_Y*TIME - (G/2.0)*(TIME**2);
end;
```

This procedure has the following general form

```
procedure COMPUTE_RISE (parameters) is
   -- local declarations
begin
   -- local statements
end;
```

The parameters of a procedure each have a mode, defined as follows:

■ *in* parameters, for example V_X, V_Y, and DISTANCE, which act as logical inputs.

■ *out* parameters, for example RISE, which act as logical outputs.

■ *in out* parameters, which act as variables whose values may be updated during execution of the procedure.

If no mode is specified, the mode *in* is assumed. Within a subprogram the value of an *in* parameter acts as a constant and may not be updated.

The name of a procedure and the specification of its parameters identify the appearance of the procedure to the user. The names of the parameters are considered local to the body of the procedure. Importantly, a procedure can contain local declarations describing internal information. The statements within the body of the procedure describe its internal behavior needed to achieve the desired effect.

In form, a function subprogram is similar to a procedure subprogram, but as mentioned above is used to compute a value for use within an expression. A function can only have *in* parameters.

Consider the following function subprogram, which is based on our previous example:

```
function NET_RISE(V_X, V_Y, DISTANCE: FLOAT) return FLOAT is
   TIME, RISE: FLOAT;
begin
   TIME := DISTANCE / V_X;
   RISE := V_Y*TIME - (G/2.0)*(TIME**2);
   return RISE;
end;
```

This function has the following general form

```
function NET_RISE(parameters) return type-of-result is
  -- local declarations
begin
  -- local statements
end;
```

Observe that the type of the value returned by a function must be specified, and that the function body must include one or more return statements. Execution of a return statement terminates execution of the subprogram and specifies the value to be returned.

4.2   CALLING SUBPROGRAMS

Once a subprogram has been defined, we want to use it, sometimes from many places in a program. This is accomplished with subprogram calls.

The most familiar form of a subprogram call uses a positional notation, where the name of the subprogram is followed by a list of arguments, one for each parameter and in the same order as the parameters. For the procedure COMPUTE_RISE, we might have the subprogram call statements:

```
COMPUTE_RISE (X_VELOCITY, Y_VELOCITY, TARGET_DISTANCE, RISE);

COMPUTE_RISE (50.0, 60.0, (EDGE_POSITION + 10.0), Y_VALUE);
```

Each argument must have the same type as the corresponding parameter. This rule follows naturally from our view of types and guarantees that a procedure will not be called with arguments of incompatible types.

As illustrated in the above calls, an argument corresponding to an *in* parameter can be an expression. For *out* and *in out* parameters, the argument must correspond to a variable; the value of such a variable may be updated by execution of the procedure.

Ada offers another, less traditional, method for calling subprograms. We can explicitly state the association between arguments and their corresponding parameters. For example, consider the procedure specification:

```
procedure MERGE (NEW_ITEMS: in TABLE; ITEMS_TO_UPDATE: in out TABLE);
```

Instead of a positional call, say

```
MERGE (SOURCE_DATA, LINE_DATA);
```

we may have

```
MERGE (NEW_ITEMS => SOURCE_DATA, ITEMS_TO_UPDATE => LINE_DATA);
```

In such calls the arguments can be given in any order. For example, we may also have

```
MERGE (ITEMS_TO_UPDATE => LINE_DATA, NEW_ITEMS => SOURCE_DATA);
```

Where long parameter lists are common and have standard default values, as in general utility packages, such calls lead to another Ada feature. In particular, a default value can be specified for an *in* parameter by giving the default value in the subprogram specification. When the default value is to be used in a call, the corresponding argument can be omitted.

For example, consider the procedure specification:

```
procedure GENERATE_REPORT (DATA_FILE : in FILE      := SUPPLY_DATA;
                           NUM_COPIES: in INTEGER   := 1;
                           HEADER    : in LINE      := STND_HEADER;
                           CENTERING : in BOOLEAN   := TRUE;
                           PAGE_LOC  : in POSITION  := TOP_RIGHT;
                           TYPE_FONT : in PRINTER   := NORMAL);
```

All of the following calls are acceptable:

```
GENERATE_REPORT;

GENERATE_REPORT (NUM_COPIES => 5);

GENERATE_REPORT (DATA_FILE  => EMERGENCY_DATA);

GENERATE_REPORT (HEADER     => FINAL_REPORT_HEADER,
                 PAGE_LOC   => TOP_CENTER,
                 TYPE_FONT  => SPECIAL,
                 NUM_COPIES => 100);
```

Each call above makes use of the default values supplied in the specification. Notice again that the arguments can be given in any order.

Finally, there are procedures where certain arguments are always present, usually in a standard order, and the remaining arguments are optional. In these cases the initial arguments can be given positionally, and any remaining arguments can be listed with their associated parameter names. For example, consider the procedure specification:

```
procedure PLOT (X, Y : in FLOAT;
                PEN   : in PEN_POSITION := DOWN;
                GRID  : in BOOLEAN      := FALSE;
                ROUND : in BOOLEAN      := FALSE);
```

The following calls may be given:

```
PLOT (0.0, 0.0);
PLOT (X_MIN, Y_MIN, GRID => TRUE);
PLOT (X_MAX, Y_MAX, ROUND => TRUE, PEN => UP);
PLOT (X_MAX, Y_MAX, UP, ROUND => TRUE);
```

4.3 SEPARATION OF SUBPROGRAM BODIES

All program units (subprograms, packages, and tasks) are characterized by two parts:

- An interface, which summarizes its properties to the user

- An implementation, which describes its internal behavior

We discuss here the ability to separate the interface of a subprogram from its implementation. In particular, every subprogram can be defined in two textually separate parts:

- Its declaration, which specifies its interface

- Its body, which specifies its implementation.

The ability to separate a declaration from its body is a novel feature of Ada. The separation provides a single basis for achieving several objectives. We can consolidate the declarations of relevant subprograms with other declarative information. Furthermore, we can isolate the description of their bodies, which often are spread over many pages of text. Finally, this ability is essential for packages (Chapter 5).

For subprograms, a subprogram *declaration* gives the name of the subprogram, its parameters, and the type of any returned value. The subprogram *body* gives the local declarations and statements.

For example, consider the following sequence of declarations:

```
procedure ADD    (I: in  ITEM; Q: in out QUEUE);
procedure REMOVE (I: out ITEM; Q: in out QUEUE);

function  FRONT    (Q: QUEUE) return ITEM;
function  IS_EMPTY (Q: QUEUE) return BOOLEAN;
```

These declarations specify procedures for adding an item to a queue and for removing the front item from the queue, as well as functions for examining the front item and testing if the queue is empty. Collectively, these subprograms define a set of operations for working with queues, and their declarations can accordingly be grouped as above, in a single place.

The bodies of these subprograms can be given after all declarations and have the form:

```
procedure ADD (I: in ITEM;   Q: in out QUEUE) is
   ...
end;

...

function IS_EMPTY (Q: QUEUE) return BOOLEAN is
   ...
end;
```

Notice that the parameter specifications of each subprogram are repeated in the subprogram's body.

Finally, since a subprogram body thus includes the information in a subprogram declaration, the declaration need not be given unless the subprogram is called in a previously given body. This is the case for the subprograms given earlier in the text. Note however, that we can always separate a procedure declaration from its body.

4.4   OVERLOADING OF SUBPROGRAMS

There are situations where we want to define the same conceptual operation on arguments of different types. A classical case is a print operation for printing different types of values.

Consider the procedure declarations:

```
procedure PUT (X: INTEGER);
procedure PUT (X: FLOAT);
procedure PUT (X: STRING);
```

for respectively printing the string representation of an integer, floating point number, or string.

The bodies of each procedure will differ, since they are dependent on the format for printing integers, floating point numbers, and strings. The use of two or more subprograms with the same name but different types of parameters is called *overloading*.

Overloaded subprograms can be called in the conventional manner, for example:

```
PUT (I + 1);            -- call for printing an integer
PUT (SQRT(Y));          -- call for printing a floating point number
PUT ("THIS MESSAGE");   -- call for printing a string
```

The key idea here is that the choice of the corresponding subprogram body is based on using the subprogram with the appropriate parameter types. Accordingly, since each of the above calls matches one (and only one) of the declarations of PUT, the appropriate body can be determined. We note in passing that this use of overloading is similar to the use of + as an operator both for integer addition and floating point addition.

Chapter 5

PACKAGES

The organization of program units is a central issue in the construction of programs. Subprograms provide one important form of organization. In particular, they allow the description of a (sometimes complex) computation that can be characterized by a simple interface to the user. As such, they provide a basic unit in program decomposition and allow for the orderly development of both small and large programs.

In this section we describe another important form of program organization, the Ada *package*. We shall see that packages can cover a wide range of uses, including named collections of common data, groups of related subprograms that collectively carry out some activity, and definitions of private types with specialized operations. Generally speaking, a package provides a service. Like any service, it may rely on internal data and services that are not (and should not be) exposed to the user.

5.1 THE VISIBLE INFORMATION

Every package is specified by giving a list of declarative information. This declarative information can be made accessible to a user, and is called its *visible part*.

Consider, for example, the following package:

```
package METRIC_CONVERSION_FACTORS is
    CM_PER_INCH: constant FLOAT := 2.54;
    CM_PER_FOOT: constant FLOAT := 30.48;
    CM_PER_YARD: constant FLOAT := 91.44;
    KM_PER_MILE: constant FLOAT := 1.609;
end;
```

This simple package defines a collection of four constants. We can readily imagine providing a more complete list of such constants, including those for areas and volumes as well as those for weights. Isolating such common declarative information in a package not only allows other program units to make use of the information, but can guarantee that the units use the same names for the constants and have the same values.

The above example illustrates the general form of all packages that only have a visible part:

```
package METRIC_CONVERSION_FACTORS is
    -- visible information
end;
```

The visible information is given as a sequence of declarations.

Even within this simple framework, there are many useful variations. For example, we may group common variables into a package such as:

```
package WEATHER_DATA is
    ALTITUDE   : array (-90 .. 90, -90 .. 90) of FLOAT;
    TEMPERATURE: array (-90 .. 90, -90 .. 90) of FLOAT;
    WIND_SPEED : array (-90 .. 90, -90 .. 90) of FLOAT;
end;
```

Just as for constants, other program units can make use of this common data, for example to read, update, or analyze the arrays.

And what about types? In a typed language like Ada, groups of constants and variables are likely to include the declaration of related types. For example we may have:

```
package GOLF_INFO is
    type GOLF_CLUB   is (DRIVER, IRON, PUTTER, WEDGE, MASHIE);
    type GOLF_SCORE  is range 1 .. 200;
    type HOLE_NUMBER is range 1 .. 18;
    type HANDICAP    is range 0 .. 36;
    type SCORE_DATA  is array (HOLE_NUMBER) of GOLF_SCORE;

    PAR_FOR_COURSE: constant GOLF_SCORE := 72;
    PAR_VALUES : constant SCORE_DATA :=
               ( 1 => 5,  2 => 3,  3 => 4,  4 => 4,  5 => 3,  6 => 4,
                 7 => 5,  8 => 4,  9 => 4, 10 => 3, 11 => 4, 12 => 4,
                13 => 4, 14 => 5, 15 => 3, 16 => 4, 17 => 4, 18 => 5 );
end;
```

This package not only defines common constants; but defines several types. Thus any units that make use of the package will also have access to the relevant types. Importantly, a user can declare constants and variables of these types, as in:

```
NEXT_HOLE  : HOLE_NUMBER;
MY_SCORE   : GOLF_SCORE;
MY_HANDICAP: constant HANDICAP := 10;
```

In all of the above examples, the effect is the same: a package specifies a collection of logically related information that can be made accessible to other program units.

5.2   MAKING USE OF THE VISIBLE INFORMATION

While a package defines a collection of information, the information is not directly visible to other program units.

One way to refer to an identifier declared in a package is with a name in the dot notation form:

package-name .declared-identifier

For example, consider the package WEATHER_DATA introduced earlier. The array WIND_SPEED can be denoted with the name

```
WEATHER_DATA.WIND_SPEED
```

and thus we might have the assignment:

```
WEATHER_DATA.WIND_SPEED(I,J) := WIND_READING;
```

Alternatively, all of the information in a visible part can be made directly visible in another program unit by giving a use clause at the beginning of the unit. For example, we may have the subprogram:

```
procedure UPDATE_WEATHER_DATA is
   use WEATHER_DATA;

   I, J: INTEGER range -90 .. 90;
   ALT_READING, TEMP_READING, WIND_READING: FLOAT;
begin
   GET_ZONE_COORDINATES (I, J);
   GET_SENSOR_VALUES (ALT_READING, TEMP_READING, WIND_READING);

   ALTITUDE(I,J)    := ALT_READING;
   TEMPERATURE(I,J) := TEMP_READING;
   WIND_SPEED(I,J)  := WIND_READING;
end;
```

The effect of the use clause is to make the identifiers declared in WEATHER_DATA directly visible in the program unit containing the use clause.

We see above that the information in a package is made visible on a selective basis. Any program unit that has need of the information can make the information visible; the other units are unaffected. Thus the identifiers declared in the visible part do not flood the name space of the entire program. In a large programming system where there might be many such packages (each offering visibility to certain information), the control and selective use of the information can provide a high degree of security.

Finally, the exact effect of packages and subprograms is quite complicated (see Chapter 8 of the Ada reference manual), mainly due to overloading, nesting, and possible name conflicts in several packages. In any case, an item declared in a package can still be denoted with the dot notation.

5.3 PROVIDING OPERATIONS OVER DATA

In our previous examples, a package provides a certain service —access to information. Data alone may not be enough. We may want to offer operations to transform the data.

As mentioned earlier, the visible part of a package contains a sequence of declarations. Recall that a subprogram can be given in two separate parts — its declaration and its body. This gives rise to the second basic form of packages, in which the visible part not only contains the declaration of constants, variables, and types, but also the declaration of related subprograms. The behavior of these subprograms is described separately in a *package body*.

A package body serves the same purpose as a subprogram body. In particular, it defines the internal details needed to implement the interface provided to the user. Like subprogram bodies, the characteristics of the package bodies are not visible to the user.

Consider the problem of defining a table management package for inserting and retrieving items. The items are inserted into the table as they are supplied. Each posted item has an order number. The items are retrieved according to their order number, where the item with the lowest order number is retrieved first.

From the user's point of view, the package is quite simple. There is a type called ITEM designating table items, a procedure INSERT for posting items, and a procedure RETRIEVE for obtaining the item with the lowest order number. There is a special item NULL_ITEM that is returned when the table is empty.

The visible part of such a package is given as follows:

```
package TABLE_MANAGER is
    type ITEM is
        record
            ORDER_NUM: INTEGER;
            ITEM_CODE: INTEGER;
            QUANTITY : INTEGER;
            ITEM_TYPE: CHARACTER;
        end record;

    NULL_ITEM: constant ITEM :=
        (ORDER_NUM | ITEM_CODE | QUANTITY => 0, ITEM_TYPE => ' ');

    procedure INSERT   (NEW_ITEM  : in  ITEM);
    procedure RETRIEVE (FIRST_ITEM: out ITEM);
end;
```

To complete the above package we need to define the implementation of the two procedures INSERT and RETRIEVE. This is achieved by defining the two procedure bodies within a package body.

A package body defining the implementation of the table management package is sketched in Example 5.1. The details of implementing such packages can be quite complex, in this case involving a two-way linked table of internal items. A local housekeeping procedure EXCHANGE is used to move an internal item between the busy and the free lists. Two local functions, FREE_LIST_EMPTY and BUSY_LIST_EMPTY, as well as local constants and variables are also used. The initial table linkages are established in an initialization part.

We see here the general form of a package body whose visible part contains subprogram declarations:

```
package body TABLE_MANAGER is
    -- bodies of visible subprograms, plus any internal
    -- information needed to implement the package
begin
    -- statements initializing the package
end;
```

While in essence the package body provides the bodies for any visible subprograms, writing such bodies may in turn require the use of local data, local types, and local subprograms. The use of local data may in turn require the execution of statements to initialize their values. These statements are executed when the package body itself is elaborated.

In general, the package body implements the service promised to the user. As mentioned before, only the visible part of the package is exposed to the user.

```
package body TABLE_MANAGER is

   SIZE: constant INTEGER := 6000;
   subtype INDEX is INTEGER range 0 .. SIZE;

   type INTERNAL_ITEM is
      record
         CONTENT   : ITEM;
         NEXT_ITEM: INDEX;
         PREV_ITEM: INDEX;
      end record;

   TABLE: array (INDEX) of INTERNAL_ITEM;
   FIRST_FREE_ITEM: INDEX;
   FIRST_BUSY_ITEM: INDEX;

   function FREE_LIST_EMPTY return BOOLEAN is
      ...
   end;

   function BUSY_LIST_EMPTY return BOOLEAN is
      ...
   end;

   procedure EXCHANGE (FROM: in INDEX;  TO: in INDEX) is
      ...
   end;

   procedure INSERT (NEW_ITEM: in ITEM) is
      ...
   end;

   procedure RETRIEVE (FIRST_ITEM: out ITEM) is
      ...
   end;

begin

   -- code for initialization of the table linkages

end;
```

Example 5.1 Package body for a table management package

5.4 PRIVATE INFORMATION

Although the mechanism illustrated above provides a simple and rich facility for abstractions, it does not guarantee the integrity of these abstractions. In our table manager example, nothing prevents a user from accessing the components of an item and changing them arbitrarily. This may be convenient, but it may also lead to serious problems, especially in applications where we wish to prevent access to data. Thus some safeguards are necessary if we wish to ensure the integrity of information. This brings up the issue of private information, in particular the use of objects whose type is specified as a *private type*.

Consider the following package:

```
package SIMPLE_I_O is
    type FILE_NAME is private;
    procedure CREATE (F: out FILE_NAME);
    procedure READ   (F: in FILE_NAME;  ITEM: out INTEGER);
    procedure WRITE  (F: in FILE_NAME;  ITEM: in  INTEGER);
private
    type FILE_NAME is range 0 .. 50;
end;

package body SIMPLE_I_O is
    -- implementation of file handling procedures
end;
```

As before, a user of this package can declare variables of type FILE_NAME, and can pass these variables to the procedures CREATE, READ, and WRITE. However, because the type FILE_NAME is declared as private, the user cannot make use of the fact that this type is internally defined as an integer, that is, the user cannot perform arithmetic on variables of type FILE_NAME. The only language defined operations that can be used are assignment and comparison for equality or inequality.

If we wish, even these operations can be forbidden by declaring FILE_NAME as a *limited* private type, as in:

```
type FILE_NAME is limited private;
```

In either case, the visible part of the package is followed by a *private part*, in which the full type definition of each private type is given. This form is characteristic of situations where we want complete control over the operations of a type.

Packages with private types serve a dual role. On the one hand, they prevent a user from operating on data of the type defined in the package. On the other hand, they implement the concept of an *abstract* data type, where the only operations over the type (aside from assignment and equality) are those given in the package.

5.5   SUMMARY

Packages, like subprograms, offer a powerful tool for abstraction. The services that packages provide range over a broad continuum, marked by three basic capabilities:

- The declaration of named collections of data and types

- The definition of a collection of related subprograms

- The declaration of data whose type properties are private.

Furthermore, with the dot notation and use clauses, a user can provide selective access to the visible information.

Chapter 6

GENERAL
PROGRAM STRUCTURE

As programs become larger, the problems in dealing with them become much larger. As a result, problems such as the organization of program units, the scope of names, the control of errors, and the difficulties of making modifications must be resolved.

In this chapter we discuss the nesting of program units (subprograms, packages, and tasks) and the visibility rules defining which declared identifiers can be referenced in a given region of program text.

We also treat separate compilation, a major facility for controlling program development. While useful even for small programs, for large programs separate compilation is central. Its basic goal is to permit the division of large programs into simpler, more manageable parts.

In discussing the Ada rules for nesting and separate compilation, a number of interrelated concepts must be introduced. In their essence, these concepts are quite simple, but their details are not. In this chapter especially, we point out the essence of these concepts and leave the details to the reference manual.

For illustration, we consider a program for solving the Eight Queens problem. The Eight Queens problem can be stated as follows. We wish to write a program to determine an arrangement of eight queens on a standard chessboard in such a way that no queen can capture any other. A chessboard can be viewed as an 8 by 8 array of squares. One queen can capture another if they are both in the same row, same column, or on the same diagonal.

For example, consider the configuration of Figure 6.1

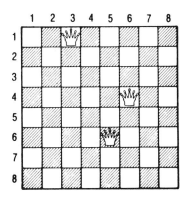

Figure 6.1 Three queens

The queen in row 1, column 3, can capture any other queen in row 1 or column 3. She can also capture the queen in row 4, column 6 because they both lie on the same downward diagonal. The queen in row 6, column 5 cannot be captured by either of the other queens. We wish our program to find one of the possible configurations in which the eight queens can be placed.

One strategy is to start by placing a queen at row 1 or column 1. Since the queen is the only one, she is safe. The next step is to find a position in column 2 where the second queen can be safely placed. A queen can be placed at row 1 of column 2, but since this queen can be attacked, the row number is incremented by 1 and the queen is tested on that square. This process continues, successively advancing a queen until a safe position in a column is found. If a configuration arises in which no queen can be safely placed in a given column, the queen already positioned in the previous column is advanced to the next row. The entire process continues until a complete configuration is found.

One small point. Two queens lie on the same downward diagonal if the difference between the row and column coordinates is the same. Similarly, two queens lie on the same upward diagonal if the sums of their individual row and column positions are identical.

A solution to the Eight Queens problem in Ada is given in Example 6.1. In this solution an array named CONFIGURATION is used to store the row positions of the queens safely placed in each of the columns 1 through 8.

Here, boolean valued arrays are also introduced. For each row 1 through 8, the array SAFE_ROW has the value TRUE or FALSE depending on whether the given row has another queen positioned somewhere in the same row. Similarly, the arrays SAFE_UP_DIAG and SAFE_DOWN_DIAG have the values TRUE or FALSE according to whether another queen exists on the given upward or downward diagonal.

```
with I_O_PACKAGE;
procedure QUEENS is
   use I_O_PACKAGE;

   MIN_ROW: constant INTEGER := 1;
   MAX_ROW: constant INTEGER := 8;
   MIN_COL: constant INTEGER := 1;
   MAX_COL: constant INTEGER := 8;

   MIN_UP_DIAG   : constant INTEGER := MIN_ROW + MIN_COL;
   MAX_UP_DIAG   : constant INTEGER := MAX_ROW + MAX_COL;
   MIN_DOWN_DIAG: constant INTEGER := MIN_ROW - MAX_COL;
   MAX_DOWN_DIAG: constant INTEGER := MAX_ROW - MIN_COL;

   FIELD_WIDTH: constant INTEGER := 3;

   SAFE_ROW      : array (MIN_ROW .. MAX_ROW)              of BOOLEAN;
   SAFE_UP_DIAG  : array (MIN_UP_DIAG .. MAX_UP_DIAG)      of BOOLEAN;
   SAFE_DOWN_DIAG: array (MIN_DOWN_DIAG .. MAX_DOWN_DIAG)  of BOOLEAN;
   CONFIGURATION : array (MIN_COL .. MAX_COL)             of INTEGER;

   ROW: INTEGER;
   COL: INTEGER;

   procedure CLEAR_THE_BOARD is
   begin
      SAFE_ROW       := (MIN_ROW .. MAX_ROW            => TRUE);
      SAFE_UP_DIAG   := (MIN_UP_DIAG .. MAX_UP_DIAG    => TRUE);
      SAFE_DOWN_DIAG := (MIN_DOWN_DIAG .. MAX_DOWN_DIAG => TRUE);
   end;

   procedure SET_QUEEN (ROW, COL: in INTEGER) is
   begin
      SAFE_ROW(ROW)            := FALSE;
      SAFE_UP_DIAG(ROW + COL)  := FALSE;
      SAFE_DOWN_DIAG(ROW - COL) := FALSE:
      CONFIGURATION(COL)       := ROW;
   end;

   procedure REMOVE_QUEEN (ROW, COL: in INTEGER) is
      VACANT : constant INTEGER := 0;
   begin
      SAFE_ROW(ROW)            := TRUE;
      SAFE_UP_DIAG(ROW + COL)  := TRUE;
      SAFE_DOWN_DIAG(ROW - COL) := TRUE;
      CONFIGURATION(COL)       := VACANT;
   end;
```

Example 6.1   A solution to the Eight Queens problem

```
    function IS_SAFE(ROW, COL: in INTEGER) return BOOLEAN is
    begin
       if SAFE_ROW(ROW) and SAFE_UP_DIAG(ROW + COL)
       and SAFE_DOWN_DIAG(ROW - COL) then
          return TRUE;
       else
          return FALSE;
       end if;
    end;

begin   -- Main Program
   ROW := 1;
   COL := 1;
   CLEAR_THE_BOARD;
   PUT ("PROGRAM TO SOLVE THE EIGHT QUEENS PROBLEM");

   while (COL <= MAX_COL) loop
      while (ROW <= MAX_ROW) and (COL <= MAX_COL) loop
         if IS_SAFE(ROW, COL) then
            SET_QUEEN (ROW, COL);
            COL := COL + 1;
            ROW := 1;
         else
            ROW := ROW + 1;
         end if;
      end loop;

      if (ROW = MAX_ROW + 1) then
         COL := COL - 1;
         ROW := CONFIGURATION(COL);
         REMOVE_QUEEN (ROW, COL);
         ROW := ROW + 1;
      end if;
   end loop;

   PUT ("SAFE QUEENS CAN BE PLACED IN SUCCESSIVE ROWS:");
   NEW_LINE;
   for I in MIN_COL .. MAX_COL loop
      PUT (CONFIGURATION(I), FIELD_WIDTH);
   end loop;
end;
```

Example 6.1   continued

6.1 ELABORATION OF DECLARATIONS

In Ada, the process by which a declaration achieves its effect is called *elaboration*. In general, a declarative part does not have a purely static meaning. For example, expressions can appear in declarations and may have side-effects or a package body may have an initialization part. Thus the full meaning of a declaration requires a careful definition, expressed by the concept of elaboration.

The most pervasive underlying principle is that of *linear elaboration*. Consider the sequence of declarations

```
MIN_ROW : constant INTEGER  := 1;
MAX_ROW : constant INTEGER  := 8;
SAFE_ROW: array (MIN_ROW .. MAX_ROW) of BOOLEAN
```

Here, elaboration of MIN_ROW and MAX_ROW allows the use of these constants in the declaration of the array SAFE_ROW.

More generally, a declarative part can contain various constituents, for example type declarations, variable declarations, use clauses, subprogram bodies, and so on. This gives rise to the rule of linear elaboration:

■ The constituents of a declarative part are processed in sequential order.

One consequence of this rule is that, once a name is introduced, it can be used in subsequent declarations in the same declarative part.

6.2 NESTING AND VISIBILITY

Observe in Example 6.1 that programs and subprograms can contain declarative parts, which may in turn contain declarations and bodies of other subprograms. This textual embedding or program units is called *nesting*.

Nesting serves several programming objectives. Most importantly, it allows a logical organization for program units. An analogy may be made with an encyclopedia, where the materials are organized into subjects and subsubjects. Accordingly, related units can be grouped and maintained together, at the level where they are needed.

Nesting also allows us to give local names for locally declared objects, independently of any outer use of the names. Thus the programmer can devise names for items without the need to keep the names of objects at different levels distinct. Finally, nesting allows us to share the visibility to common information given in outer declarative parts.

In Example 6.1, for instance, we have the general structure:

```
with I_O_PACKAGE;
procedure QUEENS is
   use I_O_PACKAGE;

   -- declaration of global constants
   -- declaration of global arrays
   -- declaration of ROW and COL

   procedure CLEAR_THE_BOARD is

      . . .

   end;

   procedure SET_QUEEN (parameters) is

      . . .

   end;

   procedure REMOVE_QUEEN (parameters) is

      . . .

   end;

   function IS_SAFE (parameters) return BOOLEAN is

      . . .

   end;

begin
   -- statements for the main program
end;
```

The main program, the procedure QUEENS, contains four nested subprograms. Each subprogram provides some conceptual operation used in the statement part of the main program.

Notice that the parameter names ROW and COL are considered as local to the procedures in which they are given. Notice also that the constant VACANT in procedure REMOVE_QUEEN is also considered as local to the procedure. On the other hand, the four board status arrays declared in the outer procedure QUEENS are used in the four nested subprograms.

This example illustrates two fundamental rules about nesting:

■ Items declared within a program unit are local to the unit.

■ A reference to an item not declared within a program unit refers to the item declared in the nearest enclosing unit.

Notice that as a result of nesting, a program unit may declare a new meaning for an identifier that happens to be also declared in an outer unit. Within the nested unit, the identifier is associated with new meaning. Thus the meaning associated with an identifier is always given by the innermost available declaration of the identifier.

Subprograms may also contain packages, and in these cases the visibility rules need to be extended. In particular, once a package is declared, its visible part is available to other program units. This may be achieved by means of a use clause in some following program unit, or by using the dot notation.

Furthermore, the body of a package has direct visibility to its visible part. In this case, the visible part of the package and the declarative part of its body are considered as a single declarative part.

For packages, there is little need to nest one package within another, although in these cases similar rules apply. That is, an inner package may contain locally declared items, and items not declared locally refer to items in an outer package.

6.3   SEPARATE COMPILATION

In the development of a large scale program we would probably make use of several packages and numerous procedures. This brings up the first basic rule of separate compilation:

- Subprograms and packages may be compiled separately.

In our discussion of subprograms (Chapter 4) and packages (Chapter 5), we noted that all program units can be specified in two parts: (a) a declaration, summarizing the calling conventions of a unit, and (b) a body, specifying the implementation. This leads to the second basic rule:

- The body of a program unit can be compiled as a separate compilation unit.

This applies to both subprogram bodies and package bodies.

Consider the program of Example 6.2, a revised solution to the Eight Queens problem. This program is compiled in three units, indicated by the broken lines separating the three units.

One unit, a procedure, defines the computations needed to solve the eight queens problem. This procedure makes use of the package QUEENS_PACKAGE, and is in effect the main program.

A second unit, named QUEENS_PACKAGE, is a package declaration for a package of generally usable constants, variables, and procedures. Notice that the visible part of this package only names those items that are of interest to the user. In particular, no mention is made of the curious convention for determining if two queens are on the same diagonal.

A third unit defines the body of the package QUEENS_PACKAGE. Notice here that the declarations of the arrays for testing the status of the queens is part of this body. Such a representation is not visible to the user, the main program.

The broken lines between compilation units are here to remind the reader that these units need not be contiguous texts. The compilation units collectively define a single programming system and hence are said to form a *program library*.

6.4   USING SEPARATE COMPILATION

As mentioned above, in a large program we will normally want to define subprograms and packages to be used by several program units. The name of a separately compiled program unit can be made visible to another compilation unit by including the name of the program unit in a *context clause* (also called a *with clause*) for the given compilation unit.

In Example 6.2 for instance, consider the unit:

```
package QUEENS_PACKAGE is
   . . .
end;
```

This package is a stand-alone collection of data and subprograms, and thus has no visibility list. On the other hand, the package can be made accessible to other units, for example in the main procedure:

```
with I_O_PACKAGE, QUEENS_PACKAGE;
procedure QUEENS is
   . . .
end;
```

Here the context clause names each visible program unit. Notice that the package I_O_PACKAGE is also included in the with clause, since the main program also uses the predefined input-output procedures PUT and GET. Both of these cases illustrate a general point. Subprograms and packages can be developed separately, and then selectively made available to other separately-developed compilation units.

We need to submit the compilation units of a program library in an order that is understandable to a compiler. Otherwise, we would like as much freedom as possible.

The rules for the order in which compilation units must be compiled follow directly from the visibility rules.

■   A compilation unit may only be compiled after all units that are mentioned in its context clause have been compiled.

Otherwise, the order of compilation is arbitrary, and can be left to the programmer.

The effect of this simple rule can be illustrated with the program of Example 6.2. For example:

1. The package declaration QUEENS_PACKAGE must be compiled before the main procedure QUEENS.

2. The package declaration QUEENS_PACKAGE must be compiled before its body.

```
package QUEENS_PACKAGE is
   MIN_ROW: constant INTEGER := 1;
   MAX_ROW: constant INTEGER := 8;
   MIN_COL: constant INTEGER := 1;
   MAX_COL: constant INTEGER := 8;

   CONFIGURATION: array (MIN_COL .. MAX.COL) of INTEGER;

   procedure CLEAR_THE_BOARD;
   procedure SET_QUEEN    (ROW, COL: in INTEGER);
   procedure REMOVE_QUEEN (ROW, COL: in INTEGER);
   function  IS_SAFE      (ROW, COL: in INTEGER) return BOOLEAN;
end;


- - - - - - - - - -


with I_O_PACKAGE, QUEENS_PACKAGE;
procedure QUEENS is
   use I_O_PACKAGE, QUEENS_PACKAGE;
   FIELD_WIDTH: constant INTEGER := 3;
   ROW, COL: INTEGER;
begin
   ROW := 1;
   COL := 1;
   CLEAR_THE_BOARD;
   PUT ("PROGRAM TO SOLVE THE EIGHT QUEENS PROBLEM");

   while COL <= MAX_COL loop
      while (ROW <= MAX_ROW) and (COL <= MAX_COL) loop
         if IS_SAFE(ROW, COL) then
            SET_QUEEN (ROW, COL)
            COL := COL + 1;
            ROW := 1;
         else
            ROW := ROW + 1;
         end if;
      end loop;
      if ROW = MAX_ROW + 1 then
         COL := COL - 1;
         ROW := CONFIGURATION(COL);
         REMOVE_QUEEN (ROW, COL);
         ROW := ROW + 1;
      end if;
   end loop;

   PUT ("SAFE QUEENS CAN BE PLACED IN SUCCESSIVE ROWS:");
   NEW_LINE;
   for I in MIN_COL .. MAX_COL loop
      PUT (CONFIGURATION(I), FIELD_WIDTH);
   end loop;
end;
```

Example 6.2   Another solution to the Eight Queens problem

```
- - - - - - - - - -
package body QUEENS_PACKAGE is
   MIN_UP_DIAG  : constant INTEGER := MIN_ROW + MIN_COL;
   MAX_UP_DIAG  : constant INTEGER := MAX_ROW + MAX_COL;
   MIN_DOWN_DIAG: constant INTEGER := MIN_ROW - MAX_COL;
   MAX_DOWN_DIAG: constant INTEGER := MAX_ROW - MIN_COL;

   SAFE_ROW       : array (MIN_ROW .. MAX_ROW)             of BOOLEAN;
   SAFE_UP_DIAG   : array (MIN_UP_DIAG .. MAX_UP_DIAG)     of BOOLEAN;
   SAFE_DOWN_DIAG: array (MIN_DOWN_DIAG .. MAX_DOWN_DIAG) of BOOLEAN;

   procedure CLEAR_THE_BOARD is
   begin
      SAFE_ROW        := (MIN_ROW .. MAX_ROW            => TRUE);
      SAFE_UP_DIAG    := (MIN_UP_DIAG .. MAX_UP_DIAG    => TRUE);
      SAFE_DOWN_DIAG := (MIN_DOWN_DIAG .. MAX_DOWN_DIAG => TRUE);
   end;

   procedure SET_QUEEN (ROW, COL: in INTEGER) is
   begin
      SAFE_ROW(ROW)             := FALSE;
      SAFE_UP_DIAG(ROW + COL)   := FALSE;
      SAFE_DOWN_DIAG(ROW - COL) := FALSE;
      CONFIGURATION(COL)        := ROW;
   end;

   procedure REMOVE_QUEEN (ROW, COL: in INTEGER) is
      VACANT : constant INTEGER := 0;
   begin
      SAFE_ROW(ROW)             := TRUE;
      SAFE_UP_DIAG(ROW + COL)   := TRUE;
      SAFE_DOWN_DIAG(ROW - COL) := TRUE;
      CONFIGURATION(COL)        := VACANT;
   end;

   function IS_SAFE(ROW, COL: in INTEGER) return BOOLEAN is
   begin
      if SAFE_ROW(ROW) and SAFE_UP_DIAG(ROW + COL)
      and SAFE_DOWN_DIAG(ROW - COL) then
         return TRUE;
      else
         return FALSE;
      end if;
   end;
end;
```

Example 6.2   continued

We assume that the library package I_O_PACKAGE has been already compiled, as is normal practice.

Apart from the required ordering on compilation, there is considerable choice remaining for the programmer. In Example 6.2 for instance, the body of the package QUEENS_PACKAGE and the main procedure QUEENS may be compiled in either order.

In any programming system, corrections or program updates require recompilation of compilation units. In large systems, there may even be thousands of modifications to a program. Obviously, in recompiling a unit we may change some information that is visible to other units, and hence any unit that utilizes this information can be affected by the change.

The rule for recompilation also follows the visibility rules:

■ A compilation unit needs to be recompiled whenever a unit mentioned in its context clause is recompiled.

Otherwise, no further recompilations are required.

In our Eight Queens program for instance, recompilation of the package declaration QUEENS_PACKAGE requires recompilation of the main procedure and the package body. Recompilation of the main procedure requires no further recompilations. Similarly, recompilation of the package body requires no further recompilations.

We see here that with a suitable organization of compilation units, the effect of program changes can be tightly controlled. Moreover, a change to a given unit need not necessitate a cascade of recompilations of other units.

6.5   SUMMARY

This completes our second level of introduction to Ada. The features described thus far have analogues in many other languages, and consequently can be used for a wide range of programming applications.

In the following sections we describe features demanded by many specialized but critical applications. Often, we expand on the features already described to meet these needs.

Chapter 7

TYPES REVISITED

In Chapter 2 we discussed the basic ideas underlying types in Ada, as well as the primitive types, enumeration types, and array types. The Ada facility for types is extremely rich, perhaps richer than any other programming language. We continue our discussion here.

7.1   RECORD TYPES

A programmer must often deal with objects having a number of different components. For example, a (hypothetical) drivers license may be an object having the following components:

Driver name: a name consisting of a
  First name: a string of 10 characters
  Middle initial: a character
  Last name: a string of 10 characters

License number: a nine digit integer

Expiration data: a calendar date consisting of a
   Month of year: one of the months January through December
   Day of month: an integer from 1 to 31
   Year: an integer

Driving code: a code for a normal, limited, special, or vip license

Depending on your driving code, there may be other information, but let us also get to that later when we discuss *variant* records.

The type used for groups of related objects is called a *record* type. A record contains a fixed number of components, each of which has a name and a value. Unlike array types, the components in a record may have different types.

For example, consider the record type definition:

```
record
   FIRST_NAME    : STRING(1 .. 10);
   MIDDLE_INITIAL: CHARACTER;
   LAST_NAME     : STRING(1 .. 10);
end record;
```

This type definition describes a record structure with three components, giving the three parts of a person's name. Just as for any type definition, the definition may be named in a type declaration and used in subsequent declarations. This gives rise to the following declarations which parallel our intuitive definition of a license given above:

```
type MONTH_NAME is (JAN, FEB, MAR, APR, MAY, JUN,
                    JUL, AUG, SEP, OCT, NOV, DEC);

type STATUS is (NORMAL, LIMITED, SPECIAL, VIP);

type NAME is
   record
      FIRST_NAME    : STRING(1 .. 10);
      MIDDLE_INITIAL: CHARACTER;
      LAST_NAME     : STRING(1 .. 10);
   end record;

type DATE is
   record
      MONTH: MONTH_NAME;
      DAY  : INTEGER;
      YEAR : INTEGER;
   end record;
```

```
type LICENSE is
   record
      DRIVER          : NAME;
      LICENSE_NUM     : INTEGER;
      EXPIRATION_DATE: DATE;
      DRIVING_CODE    : STATUS;
   end record;
```

We may now declare a variable of type LICENSE, for instance:

```
PERMIT: LICENSE;
```

The basic operation on record types is component selection. For example, to refer to the driving code of PERMIT we may say:

```
PERMIT.DRIVING_CODE
```

Notice that

```
PERMIT.DRIVER
```

is also a record, so that it makes sense to say:

```
PERMIT.DRIVER.LAST_NAME
```

With component selection we can thus refer to the components of a record variable just as we refer to the components of an array. For example, we can write:

```
PERMIT.LICENSE_NUM := 022_32_5795;

PERMIT.EXPIRATION_DATE.YEAR := PERMIT.EXPIRATION_DATE.YEAR + 4;
```

Finally, just as for arrays, assignment and comparison for equality are allowed for entire record structures of identical type. For instance, if we declare

```
TODAYS_DATE, BIRTH_DATE: DATE;
```

then

```
(TODAYS_DATE = BIRTH_DATE)
```

will be true only if all corresponding components in TODAYS_DATE and BIRTH_DATE have equal values.

Just as for arrays, aggregates can be used to denote complete record values. For example, we can assign a date to BIRTH_DATE with the positional aggregate

```
BIRTH_DATE : = (JUL, 4, 1776);
```

or equivalently with the named aggregate

```
BIRTH_DATE := (MONTH => JUL, DAY => 4, YEAR => 1776);
```

Records With Parameterized Structure

A record structure can be characterized by one or more parameters, called *discriminants*. Consider:

```
type BUFFER(SIZE: INTEGER) is
   record
      POSITION: INTEGER;
      VALUE   : STRING(1 .. SIZE);
   end record;
```

This type defines a record consisting of two components, an integer and a string. The type has one parameter, SIZE, which is used to establish the length of the string. Objects of this type can be declared by giving a *discriminant constraint*, which gives a specific value for a discriminant. For example, we may have:

```
SMALL_BUFFER: BUFFER(SIZE => 100);
LARGE_BUFFER: BUFFER(SIZE => 1000);
```

Both variables are of type BUFFER. In the first case, 100 characters are allowed; in the second case, 1000 characters are allowed.

Records With Alternative Structures

As mentioned earlier, there are cases where additional information may be required when another record component has a certain value. In our license example, the driving code may indicate a special or a limited permit requiring other information. This kind of structure is handled with a record *variant*. A record type with alternative structures must have a discriminant and must include a *variant part*. The variant part gives the various substructures for possible values of the discriminant.

Consider the following revised definition of the type LICENSE:

```
type FULL_LICENSE (DRIVING_CODE: STATUS) is
   record
      DRIVER         : NAME;
      LICENSE_NUM    : INTEGER;
      EXPIRATION_DATE: DATE;
      case DRIVING_CODE is
         when SPECIAL =>
            VEHICLE_TYPE: INTEGER;
            PASSENGERS  : BOOLEAN;
            ZONE_CODE   : INTEGER;
         when LIMITED =>
            CORRECTIVE_LENSES: BOOLEAN;
            DAYLIGHT_ONLY    : BOOLEAN;
            AUTO_TRANSMISSION: BOOLEAN;
         when NORMAL | VIP =>
            null;
      end case;
   end record;
```

and the variable declaration:

```
MY_PERMIT: FULL_LICENSE(DRIVING_CODE => SPECIAL);
```

Here DRIVING_CODE is used as a discriminant, and the case structure

```
case DRIVING_CODE is
   when SPECIAL      => -- components for a special license
   when LIMITED      => -- components for a limited license
   when NORMAL | VIP => -- components for other license codes
end case;
```

defines the alternative substructures. When the value of the discriminant is SPECIAL, the information for a special vehicle type is included; when its value is LIMITED, the information for a limited permit is included. Note that a variant may be specified as null, implying that there is no additional information. In particular, when the DRIVING_CODE discriminant has the value NORMAL or VIP, the variant is explicitly stated as being empty.

Once a record variable is assigned a record value with a given discriminant value (and thus has the alternative substructure specified by the discriminant), the discriminant of this record value cannot be changed.

The components of a variant part are referenced in the same way as other components. For example, just as

```
MY_PERMIT.LICENSE_NUM
```

refers to the license number component of MY_PERMIT,

```
MY_PERMIT.VEHICLE_TYPE
```

refers to the vehicle type number of MY_PERMIT. In the latter case, of course, MY_PERMIT must have the driving code SPECIAL.

7.2 TYPES WITH DYNAMIC STRUCTURE

In many applications we need to create objects during program execution and dynamically express their relationship to other objects. Such cases typically arise when we want to treat dynamically varying collections of associated objects, for example the nodes in a network, the components of a data base, the items in a linked list, or the members of a family tree. These applications can be described with *access* types, which provide access to dynamically created objects.

Consider, for example, the following declarations:

```
type PERSON;    -- incomplete declaration
type PERSON_REF is access PERSON;

type PERSON is
   record
      NAME       : STRING(1 ..10);
      SS_NUM     : INTEGER;
      NEXT_OF_KIN: PERSON_REF;
   end record;

MEMBER, LAST_BORN: PERSON_REF;
```

We may view an object of type PERSON_REF as a reference (pointer, if you like) to an object of type PERSON, which in turn has three components:

1. A string of 10 characters
2. An integer value
3. A reference to another person

The somewhat inconvenient declaration

```
type PERSON;
```

is called an *incomplete type declaration*. This is needed to reflect the Ada rule that any item must be declared before it is referenced.

For access types, a reference to no object is denoted by *null*. For example to initialize a family with no members, LAST_BORN can be initialized as a reference to no object with the assignment:

```
LAST_BORN := null;
```

The creation of objects of an access type is accomplished with the *new* operation. Consider the statements:

```
MEMBER := new PERSON_REF(NAME       => "ADAM      ",
                         SS_NUM      => 000_00_0001,
                         NEXT_OF_KIN => null);
LAST_BORN := MEMBER;
```

The first statement creates a new object with the three components given by the record aggregate, and assigns to MEMBER a reference to this object. The second statement assigns the same reference to LAST_BORN. Notice that the third component of the object associated with MEMBER is null. This situation may be illustrated as:

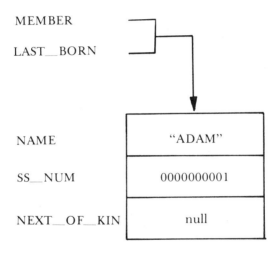

The components of access type objects are denoted in the same way as non-access type objects. For example, consider the statements:

```
MEMBER := new PERSON_REF(NAME       => "EVE       ",
                         SS_NUM      => 000_00_0002,
                         NEXT_OF_KIN => LAST_BORN);

LAST_BORN.NEXT_OF_KIN := MEMBER;
LAST_BORN             := MEMBER;
```

Here the statement

```
LAST_BORN.NEXT_OF_KIN := MEMBER
```

results in setting the third component of the object associated with Adam as a reference to Eve.

The resulting situation may be illustrated as follows:

Now that we have two persons in our family, we can see the development of dynamic relationships during program execution. The third components of Adam and Eve now refer to each other, and LAST_BORN has been maintained as a reference to the person who was last born.

7.3 DERIVED TYPES

It is not unusual to have several distinct classes of values with similar properties and operations. For example, we may wish to describe both American dollars and Swiss francs as integers, and make use of the normal arithmetic properties of integers in performing our calculations. Nevertheless, dollars and francs are distinct classes of values. Like any two distinct types, we do not want to add dollars to francs, or pass a dollar amount to a procedure expecting an amount in francs. This idea is captured with the feature for *derived* types.

Consider, for example, the type declarations:

```
type DOLLAR_AMT is new INTEGER;
type FRANC_AMT  is new INTEGER;
type YEAR_NUM   is new INTEGER;
```

These declarations introduce three distinct types. Each type has the same properties and values as the type INTEGER. For example we may have:

```
SALARY, BONUS: DOLLAR_AMT;

SALARY := 10_000;
BONUS  := 1_000;
SALARY := SALARY + BONUS;
```

Nevertheless the three types are distinct, and as for any distinct types they cannot be mixed. In particular, given

```
IMPORT_COST: FRANC_AMT;
THIS_YEAR  : YEAR_NUM;
```

we cannot have:

```
SALARY := SALARY + THIS_YEAR; -- illegal addition of dollars to a year
SALARY := IMPORT_COST;        -- illegal assignment of francs to dollars
```

In general, a type named B can be derived from an existing type named A with a declaration of the form

```
type B is new A;
```

Such a declaration means that the type B has similar values, similar properties, and similar operations as A. Otherwise the two types are conceptually distinct and cannot be mixed.

Finally, the reader may have observed that strictly speaking, dollars and francs should not really be defined as integers, since it is not really correct to multiply two dollar or two franc amounts. For defining such types in their pure form, the facility for private types (see Chapter 5) can be used.

7.4 CONSTRAINTS ON TYPES

There are of course many cases where variables have a common type but where the values that a variable can denote are kept within certain limits. For instance we may know that the value of an integer variable must lie in a particular range, or that a character variable can only denote certain characters. To handle this kind of situation, Ada has the concept of a *type constraint*.

Perhaps the most common use of constraints is for restricting the range of values for a variable. Consider the following declarations:

```
COLUMN_POS : INTEGER  range 1 .. 80;
NEXT_LETTER: CHARACTER range 'A' .. 'Z';
```

Here the variable COLUMN_POS is of type INTEGER, but its values are restricted to 1 through 80. The variable NEXT_LETTER is of type CHARACTER, but its values are restricted to alphabetic letters.

Range constraints can be applied to any scalar type, including user-defined enumeration types and real types. For example, we may have:

```
WORK_DAY: DAY range MON .. FRI;
REST_DAY: DAY range SAT .. SUN;
```

```
WEIGHT: FLOAT range 0.0 .. 300.0;
HEIGHT: FLOAT range 0.0 .. 7.0;
```

In addition to making a programmer's intent clearer, the major use of constraints is for the greater security of assignment. Constraint violations are reported at execution time by raising an exception condition (see Chapter 10). A constraint specification guarantees that any inadvertant computation producing a constraint error will be detected at the point of violation.

The use of constraints is quite general and can be applied to other basic types in the language. As mentioned earlier, for records, if a record type contains discriminants, a discriminant constraint is used to constrain a record variable to a specified variant. For example, if a license permit has a special driving code, this information can be stated as:

```
MY_PERMIT: FULL_LICENSE(DRIVING_CODE => SPECIAL);
```

Here the constraint is expressed in the form of an incomplete record aggregate where values are provided only for discriminants.

While the ability to specify constraints on types is indeed useful, knowledge about the sharing of special properties should be isolated. For example, consider the variable declarations

```
LEADING_CHAR   : CHARACTER range 'A' .. 'Z';
MIDDLE_INITIAL : CHARACTER range 'A' .. 'Z';
```

which might appear in two widely separated places within a program. The two variables above have the same type and the same constraint, yet this information is repeated twice.

Just as knowledge about types can be isolated and named in a type declaration, a *subtype* declaration can be used to factor and name the constraints on a type. Consider the following declarations:

```
subtype LETTER is CHARACTER range 'A' .. 'Z';

LEADING_CHAR  : LETTER;
MIDDLE_INITIAL: LETTER;
```

The subtype LETTER serves as an abbreviation for the type CHARACTER and the constraint that the character must be an alphabetic letter. It is important to note here that a subtype does not introduce a new type. The type denoted by a subtype is obtained from the type or subtype indication following the *is*. For example, in

```
subtype LETTER     is CHARACTER range 'A' .. 'Z';
subtype HEX_LETTER is LETTER     range 'A' .. 'F';

NEXT_CHAR: HEX_LETTER;
```

the type of LETTER is CHARACTER, and the type of HEX_LETTER is also CHARACTER. Hence the type of NEXT_CHAR is CHARACTER.

We can now show the definition of the predefined type STRING and use it to illustrate another form of constraints, index constraints:

```
subtype POSITIVE is INTEGER range 1 .. INTEGER'LAST;
type STRING is array (POSITIVE range <>) of CHARACTER;
```

The subtype POSITIVE characterizes the positive integers and, as stated earlier, strings are arrays of characters with bounds that are positive integers. For objects of the type STRING, the actual bounds can be specified in a declaration by an index constraint. For example

```
CARD: STRING(1 .. 80);
```

specifies that CARD is an array of type STRING. In addition, the index constraint (1 .. 80) specifies that 1 is the lower bound and 80 the upper bound.

The ability to declare and name subtypes complements the ability to declare and name types. For example consider the following subtype declarations:

```
subtype WEEK_DAY       is DAY range MON .. FRI;
subtype WEEK_END       is DAY range SAT .. SUN;

subtype SPRING         is MONTH     range MAR .. JUN;
subtype ARMY_OFFICER   is ARMY_RANK range LIEUTENANT .. GENERAL;
subtype FLOOR_NUM      is INTEGER   range 1 .. 33;

subtype SPECIAL_LICENSE is LICENSE(DRIVING_CODE => SPECIAL);
subtype VIP_LICENSE     is LICENSE(DRIVING_CODE => VIP);
```

We see here the expressiveness in using subtypes to describe knowledge about types.

The difference between types and subtypes can be summarized as follows. We use types to partition different kinds of objects into distinct classes. This partitioning is very strict, since we cannot mix objects of different types. We use subtypes to describe objects with common types, but with individual constraints on their values. Objects of different subtypes of the same type can be mixed in an expression and assigned to other variables of the same type, as long as the constraints are obeyed.

Summing Up

Having completed our tour through types, we offer a few comments. The entire Ada type facility is no doubt intimidating, but very powerful. The type facility includes a number of primitive types, as well as the ability to define enumeration types, array types, and record types. Dynamically varying

structures can be defined using access types, and new types can be derived
from existing types. Moreover, a programmer can define numerous types, each
building on previously defined types, and there are few conceptual limits. Some
example type definitions are given in Table 7.1.

In general, types allow us to develop conceptual units to model real world
objects with precision and clarity. Underlying the use of types is the guarantee
that the type properties declared by the programmer will not be violated during
program execution. Furthermore, any constraint violations on the values of a
type will be reported.

Table 7.1
Examples of Types

```
-- enumeration types
type DAY     is (MON, TUE, WED, THU, FRI, SAT, SUN);
type COIN    is (PENNY, NICKEL, DIME, QUARTER, HALF_DOLLAR, DOLLAR);
type OP_CODE is (ADD, SUB, MUL, LDA, STA, STZ);

-- real types
type COEFFICIENT is digits 10;
type VOLTAGE     is delta 0.1 range 0.0 .. 10.0;

-- derived types
type DOLLAR_AMT is new INTEGER;
type YEAR_NUM   is new INTEGER;

-- subtypes
subtype WEEK_DAY     is DAY       range MON .. FRI;
subtype LETTER       is CHARACTER range 'A' .. 'Z';
subtype CHAR_POSITION is INTEGER   range 1 .. 72;

-- record types
type DATE is
    record
       MONTH_NAME : MONTH;
       DAY_NUM    : INTEGER range 1 .. 31;
       YEAR_NUM   : INTEGER range 0 .. 2000;
    end record;

type INSTRUCTION is
    record
       OPERATION: OP_CODE;
       REGISTER : INTEGER range 1 .. 12;
       ADDRESS  : INTEGER;
    end record;
```

Table 7.1 continued

```
type BUFFER(SIZE: INTEGER) is
    record
       POSITION: INTEGER;
       VALUE   : STRING (1 .. SIZE);
    end record;

-- array types
type VECTOR            is array (1 .. 100)         of FLOAT;
type COEF_MATRIX       is array (1 .. N, 1 .. N)  of COEFFICIENT;
type INSTRUCTION_STACK is array (1 .. STACK_SIZE) of INSTRUCTION;

-- access types
type PERSON;
type PERSON_REF is access PERSON;
type PERSON is
    record
       NAME       : STRING(1 .. 10);
       SS_NUM     : INTEGER;
       NEXT_OF_KIN: PERSON_REF;
    end record;
```

Chapter 8

INPUT AND OUTPUT

There appear to be three dominant strategies for handling the input and output of data in programming languages :

1. *Format specifications:* Format specifications are based upon the idea that an input or output statement has an associated format description, which specifies the layout of data values and the use of spacing. This view is used in Fortran and PL/I.

2. *Picture specifications:* With picture specifications, a declared data item has an associated picture clause describing the form that such an item would have on an input or output device. This view appears in Cobol and PL/I.

3. *Specialized subprograms:* Here the layout of data for different kinds of data items is specified in specialized subprograms. For example, we may have one subprogram to output integers, and another subprogram to output character strings. This view appears in Simula 67, Pascal, and Algol 68.

In this third view of input and output, there is no notion akin to a format or picture specification. The spacing and layout of data is handled entirely by the particular subprogram that is invoked. This is the approach taken in Ada.

8.1 PRINTING A PRICE LIST

In our discussion to follow, we consider a program to print a simple report. Example 8.1 illustrates a simple price list giving two columns of data. The first column indicates the quantity of the item sold, and the second column indicates the price of the corresponding quantity assuming a fixed unit price. Our problem is to generate this price list exactly as shown.

```
                              PRICE LIST


     ITEM CODE : 1234
     ITEM      : EASY APPLICATOR
     UNIT PRICE: $4.36



          QUANTITY           PRICE
          --------           -----

             1              $ 4.36
             2              $ 8.72
             3              $13.08
             4              $17.44
             5              $21.80

             6              $26.16
             7              $30.52
             8              $34.88
             9              $39.24
            10              $43.60

            11              $47.96
            12              $52.32
            13              $56.68
            14              $61.04
            15              $65.40

            16              $69.96
            17              $74.32
            18              $78.68
            19              $83.04
            20              $87.40
```

Example 8.1   A typical report

An Ada solution to this problem is illustrated in Example 8.2. The general idea here is that for each conceptionally different layout operation, a dedicated procedure is used. For example, if we wish to output an integer, a procedure for printing integers is invoked. This procedure may have a parameter indicating the character width of the integer.

Consider the following sequence of procedure calls:

```
PUT ("ITEM CODE : 1234");
NEW_LINE;
```

Here the procedure PUT takes an argument that is a character string and displays the string on an output device. The following procedure NEW_LINE outputs a line terminator and advances to the next line.

The exact layout control for data items is handled with parameters specifying appropriate field widths. For example, consider the following procedure call:

```
PUT (DOLLARS, 2);
```

Here an integer is printed in a two digit field. In the case where only one digit is required, the digit is right justified.

8.2 USE OF SPECIALIZED SUBPROGRAMS

The use of specialized procedures for input and output has a number of key advantages. Most importantly, we can dispense with explicit format or picture specifications and subsume input-output within an already defined feature of Ada, subprograms. Thus a programmer does not need to learn any additional language features. Furthermore, the details of input and output can be summarized in terms of a familiar abstraction, the call to a subprogram.

Another advantage with this approach is that the user will generally want to define special input and output subprograms particularly suited to an application. Such subprograms fit nicely with those that are predefined in the language.

Consider, for example, the subprogram calls:

```
SET_COL(6);        -- advance to the column 6
PUT ("QUANTITY");  -- print the given string
```

These two calls refer to input-output subprograms that are predefined in Ada. On the other hand, consider:

```
SPACE_OVER(7);      -- move 7 columns to the right
PRINT_TITLE_INFO;   -- print title information
```

These two calls refer to input-output subprograms that are defined by a user.

```
with I_O_PACKAGE;
procedure PRICE_LIST is
   use I_O_PACKAGE:

   procedure PRINT_TITLE_INFO is
   begin
      NEW_LINE(4);
      SET_COL(35); PUT ("PRICE LIST");  NEW_LINE;
      SET_COL(35); PUT ("----- ----");

      NEW_LINE(4);
      PUT ("ITEM CODE : 1234");            NEW_LINE;
      PUT ("ITEM      : EASY APPLICATOR");  NEW_LINE;
      PUT ("UNIT_PRICE: $4.36");            NEW_LINE:
   end;

   procedure PRINT_COL_HEADERS is
   begin
      NEW_LINE(2);
      SET_COL(6); PUT ("QUANTITY");  SET_COL(26);  PUT ("PRICE");  NEW_LINE;
      SET_COL(6); PUT ("--------");  SET_COL(26);  PUT ("-----");  NEW_LINE;
   end;

   procedure PRINT_PRICES is
      UNIT_PRICE: constant INTEGER := 436;
      PRICE, DOLLARS, CENTS: INTEGER;
   begin
      for GROUP in 1 .. 4 loop
         NEW_LINE(1);
         for QUANTITY in (GROUP*5 - 4) .. (GROUP*5) loop
            PRICE  := QUANTITY * UNIT_PRICE;
            DOLLARS:= PRICE / 100;
            CENTS  := PRICE rem 100;

            SET_COL(9);  PUT(QUANTITY, 2);  SET_COL(26);  PUT('$');
            PUT (DOLLARS, 2);  PUT ('.');
            if (CENTS < 10) then
               PUT ('0');  PUT (CENTS, 1);  NEW_LINE;
            else
               PUT (CENTS, 2);  NEW_LINE;
            end if;
         end loop;
      end loop;
   end;

begin  -- Main program
   PRINT_TITLE_INFO;
   PRINT_COL_HEADERS;
   PRINT_PRICES;
end;
```

Example 8.2 Program to print a simple report

The subject of specialized subprograms brings up the use of two previously mentioned Ada features that are extensively used for input and output. These are overloading and default parameters.

Overloading of Subprograms

In many input-output situations we want to define the same conceptual operation on arguments of different types. A typical case is a print operation for printing different types of values.

Consider the procedure headers

```
procedure PUT (ITEM: INTEGER);
procedure PUT (ITEM: FLOAT);
procedure PUT (ITEM: STRING);
```

for respectively printing the string representation of an integer, floating point number, or string.

The bodies of each procedure will differ since they are dependent on the format for printing the three kinds of values. As mentioned earlier, the use of two or more subprograms with the same name but different types of parameters is called *overloading*.

Overloaded subprograms can be called in the conventional manner, for example:

```
PUT (I + 1);        -- call for printing an integer
PUT (SQRT(Y));      -- call for printing a floating point number
PUT ("QUANTITY");   -- call for printing a string
```

The key idea here is that these three calls are really calls to three different subprograms, each with the name PUT. The choice of the which particular procedure PUT is to be invoked by the call is determined by the type of the argument. The subroutine is chosen so that the type of its parameter matches the type of the argument.

Default Parameters

Next consider the following procedure calls:

```
PUT (DOLLARS, 2);   -- print DOLLARS with a 2-character field width
PUT (DOLLARS);      -- print DOLLARS with a standard field width
```

Here we have two calls to the procedure PUT, and in each case the value of an integer is printed. In the first case, a two digit field width is specified. In the second case, no second argument is given, in which case the integer is printed with a standard field width. The field width in the procedure is said to be a *default parameter* in the sense that if it is not provided in the call, a standard value is provided in the body of the procedure. In Ada, the standard width of an integer is the length of its decimal representation.

8.3 PREDEFINED PACKAGES FOR INPUT-OUTPUT

The complete Ada facility for input and output is expressed by a number of predefined packages (see Chapter 14, reference manual). These are

- The generic packages SEQUENTIAL_IO and DIRECT_IO
- The package TEXT_IO
- The package LOW_LEVEL_IO

The packages SEQUENTIAL_IO and DIRECT_IO define a set of input and output primitives applicable to files. The package TEXT_IO, of primary interest to us here, defines the primitives for input and output in human readable form. The package LOW_LEVEL_IO defines operations acting on physical devices.

To use these packages, you must know how to "instantiate a generic", which means that you have to provide parameters to complete its definition. In general, a *generic* program unit is a template for a class of program units. As such, generic units cannot be used directly. Instead, instances (or copies) are obtained by generic instantation.

Consider, for instance, the generic package SEQUENTIAL_IO. This package defines a collection of subprograms for working with files of a single type. To use the package for a given type, the type must be provided by the user, as in:

```
package CHAR_I_O is new SEQUENTIAL_IO (CHARACTER);
```

This is a package declaration for a package named CHAR_I_O. This package is derived from the predefined package INPUT_OUTPUT, using CHARACTER as the type of the file elements.

The predefined package TEXT_IO is a package whose visible part contains subprograms for layout control (such as SET_COL and NEW_LINE) and subprograms for input-output of characters and strings (such as PUT and GET).

The visible part of the package TEXT_IO itself contains several *generic* packages for input-output of other types (such as PUT and GET for numeric types). In particular, it contains the generic packages:

```
INTEGER_IO
FLOAT_IO
FIXED_IO
ENUMERATION_IO
```

To make actual use of these packages, the user must provide a generic instantion giving a specific integer, floating point, fixed point, or enumeration type. For instance, we may have

```
package INT_I_O  is new INTEGER_IO(INTEGER);
package COIN_I_O is new ENUMERATION_IO(COIN);
```

After such instantiation and appropriate use clauses, PUT and GET can be applied to values of type INTEGER or COIN.

It is likely that an implementation of Ada will have its own input-output package, and that is what we have assumed in this Introduction to Ada. Consider the sketch of our simple price list program:

```
with I_O_PACKAGE;
procedure PRICE_LIST is
   use I_O_PACKAGE;
   ...
end;
```

Here I_O_PACKAGE is assumed to have definitions of subprograms for input-output of characters, strings, objects of type INTEGER, and objects of type FLOAT. Using only the predefined version of Ada, this would be equivalent to

```
with TEXT_IO;
procedure PRICE_LIST is
   use TEXT_IO;
   package INT_I_O   is new INTEGER_IO(INTEGER);
   package FLOAT_I_O is new FLOAT_IO(FLOAT);
   use INT_I_O, FLOAT_I_O;
   ...
end;
```

which for simplicity, we have avoided in this introduction to Ada.

Note

This completes our preliminary discussion of input and output in Ada. Obviously, much more could be said, but by and large you should now have a reasonable start on how it all works. For the rest see Chapter 14 of the reference manual.

Chapter 9

PARALLEL PROCESSING

We are all familiar with events that can take place concurrently with other, perhaps related, events. The operation of several moving trains on a rail network, the handling of multiple lines of customers at a bank, and the simultaneous operation of multiple devices in a computing system are typical examples. The facilities for parallel processing provide a conceptual framework for dealing with such problems.

Our discussion here will make frequent use of a single example. We wish to write a program to decode messages. Let us not worry about what the messages mean. They are generated at some remote field stations, decoded, and then printed on a line printer. In particular, we wish to define three program units, named GENERATE_CODES, DECODE, and PRINT_MESSAGES:

- GENERATE_CODES: This program unit reads encoded data from several sources, and passes them on, code by code.

- DECODE: This program unit receives codes, decodes them, by some method that does not concern us here, and transmits the decoded characters.

- PRINT_MESSAGES: This program unit receives characters, and when it obtains a full line of text, displays the line on a printer.

The codes are assumed to be represented as characters.

The important point about our program is that the three program units are conceptually independent and can progress at their own rates. Except at specific points of synchronization (for instance, a message must be decoded before it can be printed), how the execution of the individual statements of the program units is interleaved in time is of no concern.

9.1   TEXTUAL APPEARANCE OF A TASK

A *task* is a program unit that can be executed concurrently with other program units. In form, a task is very similar to a package. Indeed, both a task and a package provide an encapsulation of a service. The major difference between the two is that the body of a task is not executed until the task is activated by another program unit. A task can also contain *entries*. Entries externally look like procedures, but when entries are called they specify synchronization and communication between a calling and a called task.

Consider the following sketch of the task for decoding characters:

```
task DECODE is
   entry SEND_CODE   (C: in  CHARACTER);
   entry RECEIVE_CHAR(C: out CHARACTER);
end;

task body DECODE is
   -- local declarations
begin
   -- statements for decoding characters
end;
```

This task has two entries, SEND_CODE and RECEIVE_CHAR. Just as for a package with two visible procedures, another task can issue a call to one of these two entries by means of an entry call statement. The behavior of the task, as well as the effect of an entry call, is specified in the task body. We defer the details of the body for a little later.

A task can have an empty visible part, that is, offer no service to other units. Such a task can, of course, be executed concurrently with other tasks. It can also utilize the services of other tasks. Consider the task GENERATE_CODES:

```
task GENERATE_CODES;

task body GENERATE_CODES is
   -- local declarations
begin
   -- statements for generating character codes
end;
```

and PRINT_MESSAGES:

```
task PRINT_MESSAGES;

task body PRINT_MESSAGES is
    -- local declarations
begin
    -- statements for printing characters
end;
```

These tasks have no visible part, but can be executed concurrently with each other and the task DECODE. As we shall see, they can also make calls to the entries of the task DECODE.

A Note on Task Types

As mentioned above, tasks are declared in a form similar to that of packages, that is with a declaration of its visible part and with a body. Moreover, a task declaration may specify a task *type*, and objects of such a type may be declared in the usual manner. Objects of a task type may not be assigned or compared for equality, although they can be components of arrays or records, as well as arguments to a subprogram.

For instance, we can describe a task type PRINTER as

```
task type PRINTER;

task body PRINTER is
    -- local declarations
begin
    -- statements for printing characters
end;
```

and declare our task PRINT_MESSAGES as a task object of this type, as in the object declaration:

```
PRINT_MESSAGES: PRINTER;
```

As far as the Ada reference manual is concerned, the behavior of tasks is described assuming that tasks are declared using a task type. When tasks are declared as in our decoding example, that is without types, an *implicit* task type is assumed and an *implicit* declaration of a task object of this type is assumed to follow.

In our decoding example, as well as in our general discussion of tasks, we will not have a need for explicit task types.

9.2 ORGANIZATION OF MULTIPLE TASKS

We recall from our discussion of packages that on entry into a program unit containing a package, the package body (if any) is elaborated at once in order to initialize the package. Thereafter, the package is purely *passive* in the sense that no further statements are executed unless one of its visible subprograms is explicitly called.

On the other hand, on entry into a program unit containing a task declaration, the task body is activated before executing the first statement following the declarative part. Thereafter the task is *active* in the sense that it can continue execution in parallel with the program unit that declared it and any other initiated tasks.

Thus to organize multiple tasks we need to declare task objects in a program unit. Consider the following sketch, that of our program for decoding messages:

```
procedure MESSAGE_DECODING is

   task GENERATE_CODES;
   task DECODE is
      entry SEND_CODE    (C:  in   CHARACTER);
      entry RECEIVE_CHAR(C:  out  CHARACTER);
   end;
   task PRINT_MESSAGES;

   -- bodies for the tasks

begin

   PUT ("TASKS FOR MESSAGE DECODING HAVE BEEN ACTIVATED");

end;
```

Elaboration of the three tasks results in activation of the bodies of each named task. The bodies can be executed in parallel with each other and with the body of the initiating procedure.

As far as termination is concerned, a task will normally terminate on reaching the end of the task body. When the unit containing the declaration of the task reaches its end, it will wait until all dependent tasks have terminated (unless of course, they have already done so). In our example above, the main procedure will wait at its end for the three dependent tasks GENERATE_CODES, DECODE, and PRINT_MESSAGES to terminate.

In the above discussion we have treated the notion of several tasks executing in parallel. This is essentially a conceptual viewpoint. Whether tasks are physically executed in parallel depends on the underlying implementation. In a system with multiple processors, actual parallel execution may occur. In a system with a single processor, only one task can really be active at a given time.

9.3 COMMUNICATION BETWEEN TASKS

In any system with related tasks, there must be some form of communication. We clearly do not want the trains on a rail network to collide, we may want to ensure that two bank tellers do not make conflicting transactions on the same account, or we may need to coordinate the actions of the devices in a computing system.

The basic form of communication between tasks is through calls to an entry. Consider the body for the task GENERATE_CODES

```
task body GENERATE_CODES is
   NEXT_CODE: CHARACTER;
begin
   loop
      -- statements for receiving data
      -- and generating a value for NEXT_CODE

      DECODE.SEND_CODE (NEXT_CODE);   -- entry call
   end loop;
end;
```

and for the task PRINT_MESSAGES:

```
task body PRINT_MESSAGES is
   LINE_SIZE    : constant INTEGER := 72;
   NEXT_CHAR    : CHARACTER;
   LINE_POSITION: INTEGER;
   LINE         : STRING(1 .. LINE_SIZE);
begin
   LINE_POSITION := 1;
   loop
      DECODE.RECEIVE_CHAR (NEXT_CHAR);   -- entry call
      LINE(LINE_POSITION) := NEXT_CHAR;
      if LINE_POSITION < LINE_SIZE then
         LINE_POSITION := LINE_POSITION + 1;
      else
         PRINT (LINE);
         LINE_POSITION := 1;
      end if;
   end loop;
end;
```

Both of these tasks loop forever, respectively generating codes and printing text. (Note: we shall put a stop button in later).

Here we also have the two entry calls:

```
DECODE.SEND_CODE (NEXT_CODE);
DECODE.RECEIVE_CHAR (NEXT_CHAR);
```

As we see, an entry call has the same form as a procedure call. The difference lies in their internal behavior.

For procedures, the corresponding actions (given by the procedure body) are executed when the procedure is called. For entries, the corresponding actions (given by an accept statement) are executed by the task containing the entry. Moreover, the actions are only executed when the called task is prepared to accept the entry call. Thus the calling and the called tasks may be considered as meeting in a *rendezvous*.

To illustrate this behavior, we complete our example with the task body for DECODE:

```
task body DECODE is
    CODE, CHAR: CHARACTER;
begin
    loop
        accept SEND_CODE (C: in CHARACTER) do
            CODE := C;
        end;

        -- statements for decoding the value of CODE
        -- and producing the decoded value in CHAR

        accept RECEIVE_CHAR (C: out CHARACTER) do
            C := CHAR;
        end;
    end loop;
end;
```

This task also loops forever, repeatedly obtaining a code by means of an entry call to SEND_CODE, applying the decoding algorithm, and transmitting the decoded value upon a call to RECEIVE_CHAR.

Our interest here lies in the accept statements corresponding to entry calls. An accept statement has the partial appearance of a procedure body. The accept statement repeats the formal part of the entry specification, which is followed by the statements to be executed during the rendezvous. These statements are delimited by *do* and *end* and are the region of text in which the parameters of the entry are accessible.

There are two possibilities for a rendezvous, according to whether the calling task issues a calling statement such as

```
DECODE.SEND_CODE (NEXT_CODE);
```

before or after a corresponding accept statement is reached by the called task DECODE. Whichever gets there first waits for the other. When the rendezvous is achieved the arguments of the entry call are passed to the called task; the caller is then temporarily suspended until the called task completes the statements embraced by *do* and *end*; and any out parameters are then passed back to the caller. Finally both tasks again proceed independently of each other.

We thus see the three basic notions achieved with a rendezvous.

■ *Synchronization:* The calling task must issue an entry call, and the called task must reach a corresponding accept statement.

■ *Exchange of Information:* The entry can have parameters, and thus receive or transmit values.

■ *Mutual Exclusion:* If two or more tasks call the same entry, only one call can be accepted at a time.

Notice that the rendezvous is named in one direction only. The calling task must know the name of the task containing the entry. The called task, on the other hand, will accept calls from any task. Thus in general we have a many-to-one pattern of communication. As a consequence, each entry may have a queue of tasks calling it. Any such calls are processed in the order of arrival.

It should be observed that a task can only handle one entry at a time. Although not illustrated by our example, there can be several accept statements for a given entry. We see here a sharp distinction between entries and procedures. All calls of a procedure execute the same body, whereas calls of entries need not.

We now review the complete program for our decoding problem. The program is given in Example 9.1. The main procedure MESSAGE_DECODING starts the action by declaring the three tasks. The three tasks operate quite independently, but are, of course, synchronized through the calls to the entries of DECODE. As given, the three tasks operate forever. Thus the program never terminates.

9.4 CHOOSING AMONG ALTERNATIVE ENTRY CALLS

In our decoding task above, a response to one entry call must always be followed by a response to a call of the other entry. In many applications this need not be the case. What if we have two or more entries and want to respond to the first call, no matter which occurs first? More generally, what if we are prepared to accept any one of several alternative entry calls?

For example, let us return to our decoding problem. Observe that once the DECODE task is sent a character code, it must await completion of a call to transmit the decoded value before it can process any more codes. We would really like the generation of codes and the printing of messages to go on much more independently.

Let us assume that the decoding process takes place relatively quickly. In particular, if our printing process is slow, we would still like to accept a burst of entry calls for new input codes. Alternatively, we would like to accept multiple

```
procedure MESSAGE_DECODING is
   task GENERATE_CODES;
   task DECODE is
      entry SEND_CODE   (C: in  CHARACTER);
      entry RECEIVE_CHAR(C: out CHARACTER);
   end;
   task PRINT_MESSAGES;
   task body GENERATE_CODES is
      NEXT_CODE: CHARACTER;
   begin
      loop
         -- statements for receiving data
         -- and generating a value for NEXT_CODE
         DECODE.SEND_CODE (NEXT_CODE);
      end loop;
   end;
   task body DECODE is
      CODE, CHAR: CHARACTER;
   begin
      loop
         accept SEND_CODE (C: in CHARACTER) do
            CODE := C;
         end;
         -- statements for decoding the value of CODE
         -- and producing the decoded value in CHAR
         accept RECEIVE_CHAR (C: out CHARACTER) do
            C := CHAR;
         end;
      end loop;
   end;
   task body PRINT_MESSAGES is
      LINE_SIZE    : constant INTEGER := 72
      NEXT_CHAR    : CHARACTER;
      LINE_POSITION: INTEGER;
      LINE         : STRING(1..LINE_SIZE);
   begin
      LINE_POSITION := 1;
      loop
         DECODE.RECEIVE_CHAR (NEXT_CHAR);
         LINE(LINE_POSITION) := NEXT_CHAR;
         if LINE_POSITION < LINE_SIZE then
            LINE_POSITION := LINE_POSITION +1;
         else
            PRINT (LINE);
            LINE_POSITION := 1;
         end if;
      end loop;
   end;
begin
   PUT ("TASKS FOR MESSAGE DECODING HAVE BEEN ACTIVATED.")
end;
```

Example 9.1   A solution to the decoding problem

entry calls for printing already received codes while waiting for another (perhaps delayed) input code. To smooth out these variations, we can introduce a storage area for characters in the DECODE task. Most importantly for our purposes, as long as the storage area is neither full nor empty, we want to accept a call of *either* entry.

The basic mechanism for a choice among entry calls is the select statement. Consider the following sketch:

```
select
    accept SEND_CODE (C: in CHARACTER) do
        . . .
    end;
or
    accept RECEIVE_CHAR (C: out CHARACTER) do
        . . .
    end;
end select;
```

Such a statement accepts a call to either the entry SEND_CODE or RECEIVE_CHAR. In particular, when this statement is reached, one of three cases will arise.

1. Neither entry has been called: in this case the task is suspended until one of the entries is called, and then the corresponding accept statement is processed.

2. One (and only one) entry has been called: in this case the corresponding accept statement is immediately processed.

3. Both entries have been called: in this case one of the entries is accepted. The choice is determined arbitrarily — either one may be chosen.

As indicated above, we only want to accept a call of SEND_CODE if there is enough space left in the storage area. Similarly, we only want to accept a call of RECEIVE_CHAR if there are characters in the storage area. These requirements are handled with conditions that *guard* the alternatives in a select statement. Consider the following sketch:

```
select
    when COUNT < STORAGE_SIZE =>
        accept SEND_CODE (C: in CHARACTER) do
            . . .
        end;
or
    when COUNT > 0 =>
        accept RECEIVE_CHAR (C: out CHARACTER) do
            . . .
        end;
end select;
```

The only entries that can be accepted above are those whose guarding conditions evaluate to true. Finally, we note that as before, an accept statement may be followed by statements to be executed after the rendezvous.

All of the above points are illustrated in Example 9.2, a revised version of the DECODE task given earlier. Note here that the characters are stored in the buffer in a circular fashion. The buffer has two indices, an IN_INDEX denoting the space for the next incoming character, and an OUT_INDEX denoting the space for the next character to be transmitted. We also note that the updating of the values of IN_INDEX, and COUNT is not done within the rendezvous. This allows the calling task to continue as soon as possible.

9.5   SPECIFYING DELAYS

The ability to delay a task for a specified time interval is important to many applications. We may want to stop execution for an interval of time. Alternatively, we may want to wait for some event to happen, and if the event does not take place within some required time interval, take some different action. Both of these cases are handled by a delay statement.

For example, consider the delay statement:

```
delay 10.0;   -- delay 10.0 seconds
```

The expression following delay represents the number of seconds for which the task is to be suspended. This expression is of the predefined fixed point type DURATION.

Like an accept statement, a delay statement may occur as an alternative in a select statement and may have a guard in the usual way. Such a delay statement is used to provide a time-out for the select statement. If no other rendezvous has occurred within the specified interval, then the statement list following the delay statement is executed. If a rendezvous for another alternative occurs before the interval has expired, then the delay is cancelled and the select statement is executed normally.

As an example, let us revisit once more our decoding program, in particular the procedure PRINT called by the task PRINT_MESSAGES. This subprogram may in fact call an entry LINE_PRINT for the printing of lines on a chain printer. We obviously do not want to keep the chain going if there is nothing to be printed, especially if the printer may be idle for a considerable period of time. On the other hand, if the printer has been idle, we may need to wait a second for the chain to be fully activated.

```
task body DECODE is

   STORAGE_SIZE        : constant INTEGER := 500;
   COUNT               : INTEGER range 0 .. STORAGE_SIZE;
   IN_INDEX, OUT_INDEX: INTEGER range 1 .. STORAGE_SIZE;
   CODE, CHAR          : CHARACTER;

   STORAGE_AREA        : array (1 .. STORAGE_SIZE) of CHARACTER;

begin
   COUNT    := 0;
   IN_INDEX := 1;
   OUT_INDEX:= 1;
   loop
      select
         when COUNT < STORAGE_SIZE =>
            accept SEND_CODE (C: in CHARACTER) do
               CODE := C;
            end;

            -- statements for decoding the value of CODE
            -- and producing the decoded value in CHAR

            STORAGE_AREA(IN_INDEX) := CHAR;
            COUNT                  := COUNT + 1;
            IN_INDEX               := (IN_INDEX mod STORAGE_SIZE) + 1;
         or
         when COUNT > 0 =>
            accept RECEIVE_CHAR (C: out CHARACTER) do
               C := BUFFER(OUT_INDEX);
            end;
            COUNT     := COUNT - 1;
            OUT_INDEX := (OUT_INDEX mod STORAGE_SIZE) + 1;
      end select;
   end loop;
end;
```

Example 9.2 Putting a buffer in the decoding task

Consider then the task PRINTER_DRIVER

```
task PRINT_DRIVER is
    entry LINE_PRINT (L: in LINE_IMAGE);
end;
```

and its body:

```
task body PRINTER_DRIVER is
    LINE        : LINE_IMAGE;
    CHAIN_GOING: BOOLEAN;
begin
    CHAIN_GOING := FALSE;
    loop
        select
            accept LINE_PRINT (L: in LINE_IMAGE) do
                LINE := L;
            end;
            if not CHAIN_GOING then
                -- start the chain
                delay 1.0;
                CHAIN_GOING := TRUE;
            end if;
            PUT (LINE);
        or
            when CHAIN_GOING =>
                delay 10.0;
                -- stop the chain
                CHAIN_GOING := FALSE;
        end select;
    end loop;
end;
```

This task contains the entry LINE_PRINT and controls the operation of the print chain in the manner indicated above.

In particular, the if statement

```
if not CHAIN_GOING then
    ...
    delay 1.0;
    ...
end if;
```

specifies the deliberate delay needed to activate the printer. On the other hand, consider the select statement:

```
select
   accept LINE_PRINT(L: LINE_IMAGE) do
      . . .
   end;
   . . .
or
   when CHAIN_GOING =>
      delay 10.0;
      . . .
end select;
```

As long as there are pending calls to LINE_PRINT, the delay statement is not activated. If no call to LINE_PRINT occurs within 10 seconds, the delay will be activated. Thus the chain will only be stopped if at least 10 seconds expire after the last line has been printed.

9.6 INTERRUPTING A TASK

On many systems we have hardware interrupts that are triggered by certain events. For example, we may wish to install a STOP button for the decoding system. If no more codes are to be produced or if for some reason we want our program to terminate, we press the STOP button and bring all the tasks to completion.

Hardware interrupts are handled quite simply by interpreting them as external entry calls. A representation specificiation (see Chapter 11) is used to link the entry with the physical storage address or register in which the interrupt is recorded.

Consider the task STOP_DECODING:

```
task STOP_DECODING is
   entry STOP_BUTTON;
   for STOP_BUTTON use 8#7060#;
end;

task body STOP_DECODING is
   accept STOP_BUTTON;
   GENERATE_CODES.STOP;
end;
```

Here we see an entry named STOP_BUTTON with no parameters. When a hardware interrupt is recorded, the statement

```
accept STOP_BUTTON;
```

will take the interrupt as an entry call. After accepting the interrupt signal, the following entry call to GENERATE_CODES will be executed and the task will terminate.

Next, consider the following version of the task body for generating codes:

```
task body GENERATE_CODES is
   NEXT_CODE: CHARACTER;
begin
   loop
      select
         accept STOP;
         exit;
      else
         -- statements for receiving data
         -- and generating a value for NEXT_CODE

         DECODE.SEND_CODE (NEXT_CODE);
      end select;
   end loop;

   DECODE.SEND_CODE (END_OF_TRANSMISSION);
end;
```

Here we see a simple select loop. As long as there is no entry call to STOP, the *else* part of the select statement will be executed and generate another code. However, when the entry call to STOP is executed, the select loop will be terminated.

After the loop is terminated, an end of transmission character is sent to the DECODE task, and the GENERATE_CODES task will terminate. The other two tasks can be readily modified so as to terminate when the end of transmission character is sent.

Our final program for the message decoding problem is given in Example 9.3. This completes our tour through tasks, and illustrates most of the features mentioned in this chapter.

```
procedure MESSAGE_DECODING is

   task STOP_DECODING is
      entry STOP_BUTTON
      for STOP_BUTTON use 8#7060#;
   end;
   task GENERATE_CODES is
      entry STOP;
   end;
   task DECODE is
      entry SEND_CODE    (C: in  CHARACTER),
      entry RECEIVE_CHAR (C: out CHARACTER);
   end;
   task PRINT_MESSAGES;

   task body STOP_DECODING is
   begin
      accept STOP_BUTTON;
      GENERATE_CODES.STOP;
   end;


   task body GENERATE_CODES is
      NEXT_CODE: CHARACTER;
   begin
      loop
         select
            accept STOP;
            exit;
         else
            -- statements for receiving data
            -- and generating a value for NEXT_CODE

            DECODE.SEND_CODE (NEXT_CODE);
         end select;
      end loop;

      DECODE.SEND_CODE(END_OF_TRANSMISSION);
   end;
```

Example 9.3   Adding a stop button to the decoding program

```
task body DECODE is
   STORAGE SIZE          : constant INTEGER := 500;
   COUNT                 : INTEGER range 0 .. STORAGE_SIZE;
   IN_INDEX, OUT_INDEX: INTEGER range 1 .. STORAGE_SIZE;
   CODE, CHAR            : CHARACTER;

   STORAGE_AREA: array (1 .. STORAGE_SIZE) of CHARACTER;

begin
   COUNT    := 0;
   IN_INDEX := 1;
   OUT_INDEX:= 1;
   loop
      select
         when COUNT < STORAGE SIZE =>
            accept SEND_CODE (C: in CHARACTER) do
               CODE := C;
            end;

            -- statements for decoding the value of CODE
            -- and producing the decoded value in CHAR;

            STORAGE_AREA(IN_INDEX)  := CHAR;
            COUNT                   := COUNT + 1;
            IN_INDEX                := (IN_INDEX mod STORAGE_SIZE) + 1;
      or
         when COUNT > 0 =>
            accept RECEIVE_CHAR (C: out CHARACTER) do
               C := BUFFER(OUT_INDEX);
            end;
            COUNT     := COUNT - 1;
            OUT_INDEX := (OUT_INDEX mod BUFFER_SIZE) + 1;
      end select;

      exit when COUNT = 0 and CHAR = END_OF_TRANSMISSION;
   end loop;
end;
```

Example 9.3   continued

```
task body PRINT MESSAGES is
   BLANK        : constant CHARACTER := ' ';
   LINE_SIZE    : constant INTEGER   := 72;
   NEXT_CHAR    : CHARACTER;
   LINE_POSITION: INTEGER;
   LINE         : STRING(1..LINE_SIZE);

begin
   LINE_POSITION := 1
   loop
      DECODE.RECEIVE_CHAR (NEXT_CHAR);
      LINE(LINE_POSITION) := NEXT_CHAR;

      if LINE_POSITION < LINE_SIZE then
         LINE_POSITION := LINE_POSITION + 1;
      else
         PRINT(LINE);
         LINE_POSITION := 1;
      end if;

      if NEXT_CHAR = END_OF_TRANSMISSION then
         LINE(LINE_POSITION..LINE_SIZE) := (LINE_POSITION..LINE_SIZE => BLANK);
         PRINT(LINE);
         exit;
      end if;
   end loop;
   PUT ("TASKS HAVE TERMINATED.");
end;



begin  -- Main program

   PUT ("TASKS FOR MESSAGE DECODING HAVE BEEN ACTIVATED.");

end;
```

Example 9.3 continued

Chapter 10

EXCEPTION CONDITIONS

In every application errors may arise. There are many sources of error, and many do not result from an incorrect program. Input data may contain values that are out of range, a hardware unit may fail, a tape may have a parity error, or a transmission line may be sporadically faulty. Often, a message is reported to the user and the program stops.

The simple termination of a program is not always desirable and in some cases can be disastrous. A pilot about to land may be using some computer controlled navigational system. Telling him that an overflow error has just caused a shutdown of the entire system is certainly the course of last resort. Such systems often have to do something plausible to keep running.

In this section we discuss the facilities for dealing with such situations. These facilities center on the concept of an *exception*. An exception is an event that causes suspension of normal program execution. Bringing an exception situation to attention is called *raising* the exception. Responding to the exception is called *handling* the exception.

To motivate our discussion, we shall explore the program of Example 10.1. This program computes the inverse for each of 20 matrices. Our interest here centers on the cases where a matrix is singular (that is, the determinant value is too small, and thus has no inverse.

```
with I_O_PACKAGE;
procedure INVERT_MATRICES is
   use I_O_PACKAGE;

   SINGULAR: exception;
   MAXTRIX_SIZE: INTEGER;
   type MATRIX is array (INTEGER range <>, INTEGER range <>) of FLOAT;

   procedure INVERT (M: in out MATRIX) is
      DETERMINANT: FLOAT;
      EPSILON     : constant FLOAT := 1.0E-10;
   begin
      -- compute the determinant of the matrix

      if (abs DETERMINANT) < EPSILON then
         raise SINGULAR;
      end if;

      -- complete computation of the inverse
   end;

   procedure TREAT_ONE_MATRIX (SIZE: INTEGER) is
      M: MATRIX (1 .. SIZE, 1 .. SIZE);
   begin
      OBTAIN (M);
      INVERT (M);
      PRINT (M);
   exception
      when SINGULAR => PUT ("MATRIX IS SINGULAR");
   end;

begin
   for I in 1 .. 20 loop;
      PUT ("ITERATION ");   PUT (I);
      GET (MATRIX_SIZE);
      TREAT_ONE_MATRIX (MATRIX_SIZE);
   end loop;
end;
```

Example 10.1   Using exceptions

10.1   INTRODUCING EXCEPTIONS

An exception is introduced by an exception declaration, which gives the name of the exception and defines its scope (that is, the region of text) in which the exception may be raised. For example, in

```
procedure INVERT_MATRICES is
   SINGULAR: exception;
   ...
end;
```

the exception named SINGULAR is introduced. This exception may be raised during execution of the procedure INVERT_MATRICES. As suggested by the name SINGULAR, the exception situation in mind is the event that some input matrix turns out to be singular.

The language itself defines situations that cause exceptions. These exceptions are the result of errors encountered during program execution. All such runtime errors are treated as predefined exceptions. These are the exceptions:

NUMERIC_ERROR   When the result of a predefined numeric operation does not lie within the implemented range or accuracy for the numeric type.

CONSTRAINT_ERROR   When a range constraint, index constraint, or discriminant constraint is violated, or when an attempt to dereference a null access value is made.

PROGRAM_ERROR   When all alternatives of a select statement with no else part are closed, when a program unit is invoked but its body has not been elaborated, and in various implementation-dependent situations.

STORAGE_ERROR   When the dynamic storage allocated to a task is exceeded, when the available space for objects of an access type is exhausted, or when a subprogram or declarative part is elaborated and storage is insufficient.

TASKING_ERROR   When an exception arises during communication between tasks.

10.2   RAISING AND HANDLING AN EXCEPTION

When an exception situation occurs during program execution, it must be brought to attention. This is achieved by raising an exception. In our procedure INVERT_MATRICES, execution of the statement

```
raise SINGULAR;
```

causes suspension of normal execution and brings the exception named SINGULAR to attention. The effect is to suspend execution of the program unit in which the exception arises.

The response to an exception will, of course, vary according to the application. The response can range from doing nothing, in which case the program will usually be terminated, to taking elaborate steps to deal with the situation causing the exception before continuing program execution.

A response to an exception is achieved by appending one or more exception handlers to the end of a program unit. When an exception is raised in the unit and normal execution is suspended, the corresponding exception handler is executed. Execution of the handler thus completes execution of the unit.

A program unit giving a response to one or more exceptions always ends with an exception part of the form:

```
exception
    -- sequence of exception handlers
end;
```

For example, we may have

```
exception
    when SINGULAR => PUT ("MATRIX IS SINGULAR");
end;
```

or

```
exception
    when NUMERIC_ERROR =>
        X := X_MAX;
        Y := Y_MAX;
        Z := Z_MAX;
    when SENSOR_ERROR =>
        X := X_AVE;
        Y := Y_AVE;
        Z := Z_AVE;
end;
```

We see that an exception handler has a form similar to an alternative in a case statement:

```
when exception-name => statements
```

Consider the simple procedure:

```
procedure GET_NEXT_POINT (X,Y,Z: out COORDINATE) is
    -- local declarations
begin
    -- Code to read sensor values and obtain the relative
    -- X, Y, and Z coordinates of a point.
    -- The exceptions NUMERIC_ERROR and SENSOR_ERROR may be
    -- raised during execution.
exception
    when NUMERIC_ERROR =>
        X := X_MAX;
        Y := Y_MAX;
        Z := Z_MAX;
    when SENSOR_ERROR =>
        X := X_AVE;
        Y := Y_AVE;
        Z := Z_AVE;
end;
```

Here we have a procedure whose execution can result in the raising of an exception and an attempt at some repair to the situation. When the exception NUMERIC_ERROR is raised (presumably by an arithmetic overflow), the parameters X, Y, and Z are assigned maximum values; when the exception SENSOR_ERROR is raised, the parameters are assigned average values. In either case, after execution of the handler, program execution is resumed right after the call to the procedure.

10.3 PROPAGATION OF AN EXCEPTION

In general, an exception can be raised in a program unit and an exception handler can be used to complete the execution of the unit. Frequently, however, a program unit will have no handler for an exception. Even when exception handlers are provided, they may not cover every exception that might be raised during execution. Furthermore, an exception handler itself may raise an exception. In each of these cases, the block or program unit is abandoned, and the exception is said to be *propagated.*

For example, consider the procedure

```
procedure INVERT (M: in out MATRIX) is
   DETERMINANT: FLOAT
   EPSILON    : constant FLOAT := 1.0E-10;
begin
   -- compute the determinant of the matrix

   if (abs DETERMINANT) < EPSILON then
      raise SINGULAR;
   end if;

   -- complete computation of the inverse
end;
```

and the calling sequence given in TREAT_ONE_MATRIX:

```
OBTAIN (M);
INVERT (M);  -- point of call to INVERT
PRINT (M);
```

The computations of INVERT may result in a too small determinant, in which case the exception SINGULAR is raised. As no handler is provided in INVERT, the execution of INVERT is abandoned and the exception SINGULAR is propagated to the statement where INVERT is called.

The predefined language exceptions can be viewed as exceptions propagated by the built-in features of the language. For example, when computing

```
X * Y
```

if the result exceeds the maximum implemented value, the exception NUMERIC_ERROR is propagated to the point where the multiplication is written. When an exception is propagated, the calling unit may, of course, provide a handler for the exception.

For example, consider the procedure TREAT_ONE_MATRIX:

```
procedure TREAT_ONE_MATRIX (SIZE: INTEGER) is
   M: MATRIX (1 .. SIZE, 1 .. SIZE);
begin
   OBTAIN (M);
   INVERT (M);
   PRINT (M);
exception
   when SINGULAR => PUT ("MATRIX IS SINGULAR");
end;
```

Here, if a call to INVERT results in the propagation of the exception SINGULAR, the exception is handled in the procedure TREAT_ONE_MATRIX. The handler prints a message in response to the exception. This completes the execution of the procedure TREAT_ONE_MATRIX, and program execution continues at the point where TREAT_ONE_MATRIX itself is called.

Observe that if any other exception is propagated from INVERT, for example a CONSTRAINT_ERROR, the exception is again propagated, this time to the point of call for TREAT_ONE_MATRIX. We thus see here the general rule regarding the propagation of exceptions: a raised exception is propagated through the sequence of invoking units until a unit provides a handler for the exception.

In the simple case where a program provides no handler for an exception and an execution error results in raising the exception, the program is ultimately abandoned. Normally, before abandoning the program, the predefined environment for an implementation will provide some response to the exception, usually the printing of a diagnostic. This is the familiar run time error message.

We now review our program to invert matrices, as given in Example 10.1. For each matrix the program reads in its values, inverts the matrix, and prints its inverse.

The computation of too small a determinant will raise the exception SINGULAR, in which case the procedure INVERT is abandoned and the exception is propagated to the calling procedure TREAT_ONE_MATRIX. This procedure in turn is suspended, but here a handler for the exception is provided. The handler simply prints the message:

```
MATRIX IS SINGULAR
```

This action completes execution of TREAT_ONE_MATRIX, and then control is returned to its point of call, where the next matrix is processed. Thus we see here the propagation of an exception and a simple diagnostic action, allowing the program to continue in case of an error.

Finally, we note that the raising of any other exception within INVERT, for example CONSTRAINT_ERROR, is propagated back to each caller. In this case the program itself is abandoned; presumably, the default environment for an implementation will give some diagnostic message.

It is possible to make our program more robust by providing a default handler for all possible other errors:

```
procedure TREAT_ONE_MATRIX is
    M: MATRIX;        begin
    READ (M);
    INVERT (M);
    PRINT (M);
exception
    when SINGULAR => PUT ("MATRIX IS SINGULAR");
    when others   => PUT ("UNEXPECTED ERROR");
end;
```

The reserved word *others* stands for any other raised exception name. Here it will catch every exception except SINGULAR. As a consequence it will be possible to process the next matrix, even with, for example, a NUMERIC_ERROR or CONSTRAINT_ERROR.

10.4 EXCEPTIONS ARISING DURING INTER-TASK COMMUNICATION

The use of multiple tasks brings up the issue of communicating program units. Of interest here is that an exception situation in one task may be relevant to another task. Faulty communication between tasks is generally brought to attention with the predefined exception TASKING_ERROR.

For example, consider the following cases:

■ a task calls an entry in another task, but the second task has already been completed.

■ a task calls an entry in another task, the second task is active but completes execution before accepting the entry call.

■ a task calls an entry in another task, the second task accepts the entry call but an unhandled exception arises during the rendezvous.

In the first two cases, the predefined exception TASKING_ERROR is raised in the calling task. In the third case, the exception is propogated to the calling task.

Finally, a task may discover that another task is faulty and that communication has become impossible. In such an extreme and abnormal situation, any task can explicitly terminate another task with an abort statement, such as:

```
abort DISK_HANDLER;
```

Such unconditional termination should be used with great caution.

Chapter 11

UTILIZING THE IMPLEMENTATION

A program does not exist alone. It must be translated into a form suitable for machine execution, and executed on a specific machine. In most cases, a high level language permits the formulation of the program in terms that do not depend on the machine. The main benefit derived from this machine independence is portability. However there are situations in which it is important to have some control over the implementation and to take advantage of its characteristics.

11.1 REPRESENTING DATA

In Chapter 2 we discussed the basic idea of types, whereby the logical properties of data are defined. Some system applications require the ability to describe the physical layout of data, either for dealing with special hardware devices or for efficiency. We turn then to the idea of *representation clauses.*

The Ada facility for representation specifications is based on two underlying ideas:

1. *Separation Principle:* Data can be specified in two steps. First, the logical properties are described using a type definition. Second, any special representation properties are described by a representation clause for the type.

2. *One Type, One Representation:* A given type of data can have only one explicit representation.

In the usual case where the programmer is not concerned with the specific representation of data, the representation is determined by the compiler.

Consider the following type declaration and associated representation clause:

```
type OP_CODE is (ADD, SUB, MUL, LDA, STA, STZ);

for OP_CODE use (ADD=>1, SUB=>2, MUL=>3, LDA=>8, STA=>24, STZ=>33);
```

In the absence of a representation clause, no assumption can be made on the representation chosen by the compiler. Here, however, the values of the enumeration type OP_CODE are explicitly defined with integer representation values.

More generally, a representation clause can be used to specify detailed bit configurations for data. For example, consider the following declarations:

```
WORD: constant INTEGER := 4; -- storage unit is byte, 4 bytes per word

type STATE is (A, M, W, P);
type MODE  is (FIX, DEC, EXP, SIGNIF);

type PROGRAM_STATUS_WORD is
   record
      SYSTEM_MASK    : array (0 .. 7) of BOOLEAN;
      PROTECTION_KEY : INTEGER range 0 .. 3;
      MACHINE_STATE  : array (STATE) of BOOLEAN;
      INTERRUPT_CAUSE: INTERRUPTION_CODE;
      ILC            : INTEGER range 0 .. 3;
      CC             : INTEGER range 0 .. 3;
      PROGRAM_MASK   : array (MODE) of BOOLEAN;
      INST_ADDRESS   : ADDRESS;
   end record;
```

Objects of type PROGRAM_STATUS_WORD can be given a specific representation as follows:

```
for PROGRAM_STATUS_WORD use
   record
      SYSTEM_MASK      at 0*WORD range  0 ..  7;
      PROTECTION_KEY   at 0*WORD range 10 .. 11;  -- bits 8, 9 unused
      MACHINE_STATE    at 0*WORD range 12 .. 15;
      INTERRUPT_CAUSE  at 0*WORD range 16 .. 31;
      ILC              at 1*WORD range  0 ..  1;  -- second word
      CC               at 1*WORD range  2 ..  3;
      PROGRAM_MASK     at 1*WORD range  4 ..  7;
      INST_ADDRESS     at 1*WORD range  8 .. 31;
   end record;
```

In each of the above cases, the form for specifying the representation of data is:

for *type-name* use *representation*;

For records, each component representation has the form:

component-name at *address* range *first-bit* .. *last-bit*;

The component address is the relative address (in storage units) with respect to the start of the record, the first bit and the last bit define the bit positions of the component within the storage unit. In the case above, for each object of type PROGRAM_STATUS_WORD, the first eight bits (bits 0 through 7 of word 0) are occupied by the component STYSTEM_MASK, bits 10 and 11 by the component PROTECTION_KEY, and so on.

There are several other forms of representation specifications in Ada. For instance, we can specify the space reserved for objects or the storage address of a variable. Each form illustrates the same general idea: the programmer can exercise some control over the characteristics of the machine on which a program is executed.

11.2   CHANGING THE REPRESENTATION OF DATA

A classical problem in dealing with data is that we may want to change the representation. For example, data stored on a given device may need to be moved to a different device, or we may wish to change data stored in a compact form into another form for more efficient processing.

The problem of change of representation is straightforward; it can be expressed as an explicit type conversion between a first type and a second type derived from the first but with different representation specifications.

For example, consider:

```
type DESCRIPTOR is
    record
        -- components of a descriptor
    end record;

type PACKED_DESCRIPTOR is new DESCRIPTOR;

for PACKED_DESCRIPTOR use
    record
        -- components of a packed descriptor
    end record;
```

Here DESCRIPTOR and PACKED_DESCRIPTOR are two different types with identical characteristics, apart from their representation. Change of representation can be accomplished with explicit type conversions. Thus with the declarations:

```
D: DESCRIPTOR;
P: PACKED_DESCRIPTOR;
```

we can write:

```
P := PACKED_DESCRIPTOR(D);  -- pack D
D := DESCRIPTOR(P);         -- unpack P
```

Here the type conversions are specified by expressions of the form:

derived-type (value)

Such a conversion accomplishes a change of representation of the value to that given for the derived type.

11.3   GIVING INSTRUCTIONS TO THE TRANSLATOR

The creation of a program involves some communication with the language compiler. For example, we may wish to state that only certain portions of a program unit are to be listed, or we may wish to specify that the code generated for a subprogram is to be inserted in line. These kinds of problems can be handled with *pragmas*.

A pragma is an instruction to the compiler. Since there may be many compilers for Ada, the allowable pragmas will generally vary from implementation to implementation. Some pragmas, for example the pragma specifying that a subprogram is to be expanded in line, are predefined for all implementations. The following examples illustrate use of pragmas that are predefined in the language:

```
pragma LIST (OFF);            -- suspend listing

pragma SUPRESS (RANGE_CHECK);  -- supress the checking
                              -- of range constraints

pragma MEMORY_SIZE (60_000);  -- the required memory is established
                              -- as 60,000 storage units

pragma INLINE (SET_MASK);     -- at each call, expand the body of
                              -- the subprogram SET_MASK in-line
```

A typical implementation may also have predefined pragmas, for example:

```
pragma TRACE (X, Y);          -- generate code to monitor changes
                              -- to the variables X and Y

pragma PROFILE (STORAGE);     -- provide a storage profile for
                              -- the program
```

In each case, the point is the same. A pragma allows the programmer to exercise some control over the characteristics of the compiler that processes a program.

11.4 ENVIRONMENT INQUIRIES

In Chapter 2 on describing data we discussed the use of the predefined attributes of a type. More generally, an attribute serves as a mechanism for obtaining information that is known to the compiler. Attributes have the form:

entity'attribute-designator

The entity is either a type or some declared entity.

There are several broad uses of attributes. One use is to refer to information about types, for example:

```
DAY'FIRST           -- the first element of type DAY
DAY'SUCC            -- the successor function for the type DAY

COEFFICIENT'DIGITS  -- the number of decimal digits specified for
                    -- the floating point type COEFFICIENT

COEFFICIENT'LARGE   -- the maximum expressible value of
                    -- type COEFFICIENT

INTEGER'SIZE        -- the implemented size of an integer in bits
```

A second class of uses refers to general information known to the compiler. For example, if PSW is a variable of type PROGRAM_STATUS_WORD, we may have:

```
PROGRAM_STATUS_WORD'SIZE   -- the number of bits specified for
                           -- representing objects of type
                           -- PROGRAM_STATUS_WORD

PSW'ADDRESS                -- storage address of the variable PSW

PSW.PROGRAM_MASK'FIRST_BIT -- the first bit of the record
                           -- component PSW.PROGRAM_MASK
```

A third class of use is for obtaining information that is known during program execution. For example, we may have:

```
DECODE'TERMINATED  -- true if the task DECODE is terminated

SEND_CODE'COUNT    -- the number of pending calls
                   -- to the entry SEND_CODE
```

In addition to language defined attributes, an implementation may introduce other implementation attributes. Overall, the facility for attributes provides a method for obtaining program and implementation dependent information.

Chapter 12

In a language as rich as Ada, one would expect to be able to write programs that are elegant and clear. Such is the case.

To illustrate the use of Ada in solving larger problems, we consider a program to format text. This is given as Example 12.1. This program reads lines of text, arranges the text to fill each line properly, and prints the resulting text. For instance, with the input

```
While the    criminal investigator
typically does
not consider himself a     disciple
of empirical science,
his work, like  the chemist's,
consists in a
logical and systematic
quest      for Truth.
```

the program prints:

```
       While the criminal investigator typically does not
consider himself a disciple of empirical science, his work,
like the chemist's consists of a logical and systematic
quest for Truth.
```

In addition to rearranging text, the program allows the user to include within the text certain commands to control the final appearance. For instance, a command such as

    :INDENT 10

would cause the following lines of text to be indented ten spaces. Then if one wished to return to the left margin, the command

    :INDENT 0

would suffice. Other commands allow lines to be printed verbatim, the centering of one or more lines, the insertion of blank lines, and advancement to a new page. The output pages are numbered sequentially. A more complete description of the program is given in the program itself.

Perhaps the most dominant feature of the program is the use of packages. The general structure of the program can be outlined as follows:

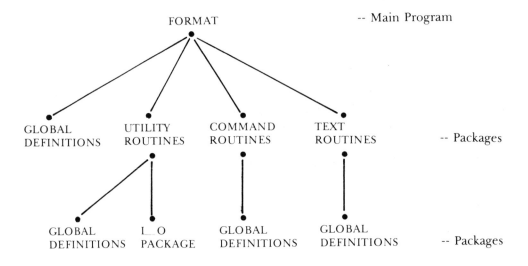

Here we see a simple main program format that makes use of four packages:

- GLOBAL_DEFINITIONS: This package is a simple collection of constants and types that are used throughout the program.

- UTILITY_ROUTINES: This package contains a number of general purpose subprograms, mainly those for input and output.

- COMMAND_ROUTINES: This package contains only one visible subprogram, that for processing command lines.

■ TEXT_ROUTINES: This package defines two visible
subprograms, one for processing paragraph lines and one for
verbatim lines.

The package UTILITY_ROUTINES, in turn, makes use of the predefined
I_O_PACKAGE assumed for this introduction. The main program, the package
specifications, and the package bodies can be compiled separately; this is
indicated by the broken lines between the compilation units.

The package COMMAND_ROUTINES deserves a special note. While this
package contains only one visible subprogram, it makes internal use of a
number of locally defined subprograms. These subprograms have a tree-like
hierachy similar to that found in other programming languages.

The Ada package organization is in considerable contrast to languages
where subprograms are the main organizational unit. This brings up a key issue
in the use of Ada. The Ada language is, in part, a new design tool for programs.
Like any design tool, the language can have a far-reaching effect on the way we
think about programs.

```
--  ** Program Title: FORMAT
--
--
--  ** Program Intent:
--      This program reads a text file and formats it according to
--      conventions given below. The text file contains lines of text
--      and command lines. Each command line begins with a colon
--      and must be followed by a legal command name.
--
--
--  ** Input and Output Files:
--      SOURCE_TEXT: A file containing text lines and command lines.
--      OUTPUT_TEXT: The formatted text.
--
--
--  ** General Layout Conventions:
--      Page Size: Standard 8 1/2 by 11 page, 85 characters per
--      line, 66 lines per page.
--
--      Margins:
--          Left  : 15 characters in from left edge of page
--          Right : 10 characters in from right edge of page
--          Top   : 6 lines down from top of page
--          Bottom: 6 lines from bottom of page
--
--      Printing Area: Standard 10 pitch spacing, 60 characters per
--      line, 54 lines per page
--
--      Page Numbers: 3 lines down from bottom margin, centered
--      between the left and right margin, and enclosed by hyphens,
--      For example
--
--                              - 14 -
```

Example 12.1 An Ada Program to Format Text

```
--  ** Commands:
--      :PARAGRAPH  Indicates the beginning of a paragraph. All
--                  following lines of text up to the next command line
--                  are treated as a sequence of words without line
--                  boundaries. The words are printed with
--                  end-of-lines inserted so that each line (except the
--                  last) will be filled with one space between each
--                  word. The first line of each paragraph is indented
--                  5 spaces. The right margin is ragged edged.
--
--                  If the paragraph is followed by a blank line or one
--                  or more commands (excluding the verbatim command),
--                  then the next line of text will be considered
--                  the beginning of a new paragraph.
--
--      :VERBATIM   Indicates the beginning of a series of lines that are
--                  to be output exactly as they are given, except for
--                  possible indentation. All lines (excluding command
--                  lines) between the verbatim command line and the next
--                  paragraph command line (or the end of input) are
--                  treated as text to be printed verbatim.
--
--      :INDENT n   Causes all following text lines to be indented n
--                  spaces from the left margin (n from 0 through 60).
--
--      :CENTER n   Causes the following n lines of input text (n > 0)
--                  to be centered between the left and right margins.
--                  If n is omitted, then only the first following
--                  line of input will be centered.
--
--      :SPACE n    Causes n blank lines (n > 0) to be printed. If n is
--                  omitted, then only one blank line is printed. Note
--                  that a blank line of text in the input is treated
--                  exactly as a ":SPACE 1" command line.
--
--      :PAGE       Causes the next line to be printed at the top of a
--                  new page. This is also done automatically whenever
--                  a page is filled.
```

Example 12.1   continued

```
--   ** Sample Input:
--
--   :CENTER 2
--   THIS IS A TITLE
--   ---- -- - -----
--
--   :PARAGRAPH
--   The text of a paragraph is  adjusted
--   on a line to fit on
--   a line with at most 60 characters.
--
--   :INDENT 10
--   One or more lines can be indented from the left margin
--   with an indent command.
--
--   :INDENT 0
--   One can also specify that line are to be printed
--   verbatim, as in the following short table:
--
--   :VERBATIM
--
--       ITEM        AMOUNT
--        1            18
--        2             6
--        3            11
--
--
--
--
--   ** Corresponding Output:
--
--                     THIS IS A TITLE
--                     ---- -- - -----
--
--       The text of a paragraph is adjusted on a line to fit on
--   a line with at most 60 characters.
--
--                 One or more lines can be indented from the
--            left margin with an indent command.
--
--       One can also specify that lines are to be printed
--   verbatim as in the following short table:
--
--       ITEM        AMOUNT
--        1            18
--        2             6
--        3            11
```

Example 12.1   continued

```
--  ** Error Conditions:
--
--     1. An input line beginning with a colon is not followed by a
--     legitimate command.
--
--        Response:  The line is output verbatim with five asterisks
--        in the left margin to call attention to the problem.
--
--
--     2. The argument given for an indent command is not numeric or
--     too large (> 60); the argument given for a center or space
--     command is not numeric or too large (> 99).
--
--        Response:  As above.
--
--
--     3. One of the lines to be centered with a center command is a
--     command line.
--
--        Response:  The line is output centered, but five asterisks
--        are placed in the left margin to call attention to the
--        problem.
--
--
--     4. A line to be output extends beyond the right margin. This
--     can be a verbatim line that is too long or a word in a
--     paragraph line that is too long (for example, if the indent
--     happens to be 40 characters, and a word will not fit in the
--     remaining 20 spaces).
--
--        Response:  Allow the line to be output up to, but not
--        beyond, the edge of the page.  Place five asterisks in the
--        left margin to call attention to the problem.
```

Example 12.1   continued

```
with GLOBAL_DEFINITIONS, UTILITY_ROUTINES, COMMAND_ROUTINES, TEXT_ROUTINES;
procedure FORMAT is
    use GLOBAL_DEFINITIONS, UTILITY_ROUTINES, COMMAND_ROUTINES, TEXT_ROUTINES;

    -- This is the main program. Its function is
    -- to determine the kind of processing for the next
    -- group of input lines.

      TEXT_MODE    : MODE;
      INDENTATION : INDENT_RANGE;

begin  -- Main Program

    TEXT_MODE    := PARGRAPH_MODE;
    INDENTATION  := 0;

    while MORE_DATA(SOURCE_TEXT) loop
       if NEXT_INPUT_CHAR = COMMAND_CHAR then
          DO_COMMANDS (TEXT_MODE, INDENTATION);
       else
          case TEXT_MODE is
             when PARGRAPH_MODE => DO_PARAGRAPH (INDENTATION);
             when VERBATIM_MODE => DO_VERBATIM  (INDENTATION);
          end case;
       end if;
    end loop;
    FINISH_PAGE;

end;
```

Example 12.1   continued

```
- - - - - - - - - - - - -

package GLOBAL_DEFINITIONS is

   -- This package defines constants and types used
   -- in the main program and the other packages.

   PAGE_SIZE       : constant INTEGER := 66;
                       -- Number of lines from top edge to bottom of page
   LINES_PER_PAGE  : constant INTEGER := 54;
                       -- Number of lines from top margin to bottom margin
   LEFT_MARGIN     : constant INTEGER := 15;
                       -- Number of columns from left edge of page to left margin
   RIGHT_MARGIN    : constant INTEGER := 60;
                       -- Number of columns from left margin to right margin
   MAX_LINE_LENGTH : constant INTEGER := 70;
                        -- Maximum number of characters per line, from the
                        -- left margin to the right edge of page


   COMMAND_CHAR    : constant CHARACTER := ':';
   BLANK           : constant CHARACTER := ' ';
   NORMAL_MARGIN   : constant STRING    := (1..15 => BLANK);
   ERROR_MARGIN    : constant STRING    := (1..5 => '*',  6..15 => BLANK);

   type MODE            is (PARAGRAPH_MODE, VERBATIM_MODE);
   type COMMAND_NAME    is (PARAGRAPH, VERBATIM, INDENT,
                              CENTER, SPACE, PAGE, ILLEGAL);

   subtype INDENT_RANGE is INTEGER range 0 .. RIGHT_MARGIN;
   subtype ARG_RANGE    is INTEGER range 0 .. 99;
   subtype COLUMN_NUM   is INTEGER range 0 .. MAX_LINE_LENGTH;

   type LINE_INFO is
      record
         LENGTH: INTEGER range 0 .. MAX_LINE_LENGTH;
         IMAGE : STRING(1..MAX_LINE_LENGTH);
      end;

   type COMMAND_INFO is
      record
         NAME    : COMMAND_NAME;
         ARGUMENT: ARG_RANGE;
         LINE    : LINE_INFO;
      end;

end;
```

Example 12.1   continued

```
- - - - - - - - - - - -

with GLOBAL_DEFINITIONS, I_O_PACKAGE;
package UTILITY_ROUTINES is
   use GLOBAL_DEFINITIONS, I_O_PACKAGE;

   -- This package defines the input and output files, the look
   -- ahead character for reading input lines, and a number of
   -- functions and procedures for input and output of the text.

   SOURCE_TEXT     : IN_FILE;
   OUTPUT_TEXT     : OUT_FILE;
   NEXT_INPUT_CHAR: CHARACTER;

   function MORE_DATA   (F: in IN_FILE) return BOOLEAN;
   function MORE_ON_LINE(F: in IN_FILE) return BOOLEAN;
   function DIGIT_VALUE (CHAR: in CHARACTER) return INTEGER;

   procedure GET_CHAR (CHAR: out CHARACTER);
   procedure GET_LINE (LINE: out LINE_INFO);
   procedure CLOSE_OUT_LINE;

   procedure PRINT_MARGIN (MARGIN: in STRING);
   procedure PRINT_TEXT (LINE: in LINE_INFO);

   procedure DO_INDENT (NUM_SPACES: in INTEGER);
   procedure START_NEW_LINE;
   procedure FINISH_PAGE;

end;

- - - - - - - - - - - -

with GLOBAL_DEFINITIONS;
package COMMAND_ROUTINES is
   use GLOBAL_DEFINITIONS;

   -- This package defines the procedure for handling command lines.

   procedure DO_COMMANDS (TEXT_MODE   : out MODE;
                          INDENTATION: out INDENT_RANGE);
end;

- - - - - - - - - - - -

with GLOBAL_DEFINITIONS;
package TEXT_ROUTINES is
   use GLOBAL_DEFINITIONS;

   -- This package defines the procedures for handling verbatim and
   -- paragraph lines.

   procedure DO_VERBATIM  (INDENTATION: in INDENT_RANGE);
   procedure DO_PARAGRAPH (INDENTATION: in INDENT_RANGE);
end;
```

Example 12.1 continued

```
- - - - - - - - - - - - -

with GLOBAL_DEFINITIONS, I_O_PACKAGE;
package body UTILITY_ROUTINES is
   use GLOBAL_DEFINITIONS, I_O_PACKAGE;

   PAGE_NUM : INTEGER;
   LINE_NUM : INTEGER range 1 .. PAGE_SIZE;
   NULL_CHAR: constant CHARACTER := ASCII.NUL;


function MORE_DATA(F: in IN_FILE) return BOOLEAN is
   -- This function determines if there are more characters
   -- on the input file.
begin
   if not END_OF_FILE(F) then
      return TRUE;
   else
      return FALSE;
   end if;
end;


function MORE_ON_LINE(F: in IN_FILE) return BOOLEAN is
   -- This function determines if there are more characters
   -- on the line being read.
begin
   if not END_OF_LINE(F) then
      return TRUE;
   else
      return FALSE;
   end if;
end;


function DIGIT_VALUE(CHAR: in CHARACTER) return INTEGER is
   -- This function determines the numeric value
   -- of a character.
begin
   return CHARACTER'POS(CHAR) - CHARACTER'POS('0');
end;
```

Example 12.1   continued

```
procedure GET_CHAR (CHAR: out CHARACTER) is
   -- This procedure obtains the next input character
   -- and maintains a one character look ahead.
begin
   CHAR := NEXT_INPUT_CHAR;
   if MORE_DATA(SOURCE_TEXT) then
      if MORE_ON_LINE(SOURCE_TEXT)then
         GET (NEXT_INPUT_CHAR);
      else
         NEXT_INPUT_CHAR := NULL_CHAR;
      end if;
   end if;
end;


procedure GET_LINE (LINE: out LINE_INFO) is
   -- This procedure obtains the next input line, and
   -- removes any trailing blanks.
   TRAILING_BLANKS: BOOLEAN;
begin
   LINE.LENGTH := 0;
   while (LINE.LENGTH < MAX_LENE_LENGTH) and MORE_ON_LINE(SOURCE_TEXT) loop
      LINE.LENGTH := LINE.LENGTH + 1;
      GET_CHAR (LINE.IMAGE(LINE.LENGTH));
   end loop;
   CLOSE_OUT_LINE;

   TRAILING_BLANKS := TRUE;
   while TRAILING_BLANKS and LINE.LENGTH /= 0 loop
      if LINE.IMAGE(LINE.LENGTH) /= BLANK then
         TRAILING_BLANKS := FALSE;
      else
         LINE.LENGTH := LINE.LENGTH - 1;
      end if;
   end loop;
end;
```

Example 12.1   continued

```
procedure CLOSE_OUT_LINE is
   -- This procedure skips over any excess characters
   -- on a line.
begin
   SKIP_LINE;
   GET_CHAR (NEXT_INPUT_CHAR);
end;


procedure PRINT_MARGIN (MARGIN: in STRING) is
   -- This procedure prints the margin area of an output line.
begin
   PUT (MARGIN);
end;


procedure PRINT_TEXT (LINE: in LINE_INFO) is
   -- This procedure prints the text of an output line.
begin
   PUT (LINE.IMAGE(1..LINE.LENGTH));
end;


procedure DO_INDENT (NUM_SPACES: in INDENT_RANGE) is
   -- This procedure handles the given indentation.

begin
   SET_COL (LEFT_MARGIN + NUM_SPACES + 1);
end;
```

Example 12.1   continued

```
procedure START_NEW_LINE is
   -- This procedure causes an advance to a new output line.
begin
   if LINE_NUM = LINES_PER_PAGE then
      FINISH_PAGE;
   else
      NEW_LINE;
      LINE_NUM := LINE_NUM + 1;
   end if;
end;


procedure FINISH_PAGE is
   -- This procedure completes the text of an output page
   -- and prints the page number.
   PAGE_NUM_COL    : constant INTEGER := 28;
   PAGE_NUM_LINE   : constant INTEGER := 57;
   NUM_BLANK_LINES: 1 .. PAGE_SIZE;
begin
   NUM_BLANK_LINES := PAGE_NUM_LINE - LINE_NUM;
   NEW_LINE (NUM_BLANK_LINES);

   SET_COL (PAGE_NUM_COL);
   PUT ("- ");  PUT (PAGE_NUM);  PUT (" -");

   NUM_BLANK_LINES := (PAGE_SIZE - PAGE_NUM_LINE) + 1;
   NEW_LINE (NUM_BLANK_LINES);

   LINE_NUM := 1;
   PAGE_NUM := PAGE_NUM + 1;
end;


begin  -- initialization for UTILITY_ROUTINES
   SET_INPUT  (SOURCE_TEXT);
   SET_OUTPUT (OUTPUT_TEXT);
   LINE_NUM := 1;
   PAGE_NUM := 1;
   NEXT_INPUT_CHAR := NULL_CHAR;
   GET_CHAR (NEXT_INPUT_CHAR);
end;
```

Example 12.1   continued

```
- - - - - - - - - - - - -

with GLOBAL_DEFINITIONS, UTILITY_ROUTINES;
package body COMMAND_ROUTINES is
   use GLOBAL_DEFINITIONS, UTILITY_ROUTINES;

   procedure CENTER_LINE;
   procedure PARSE_LINE (COMMAND: out COMMAND_INFO);
   procedure GET_ARGUMENT (LINE          : in LINE_INFO;
                           END_OF_COMMAND: in COLUMN_NUM;
                           NAME          : in out COMMAND_NAME;
                           ARGUMENT      : out ARG_RANGE);
   procedure GET_COMMAND  (LINE          : in LINE_INFO;
                           NAME          : out COMMAND_NAME;
                           END_OF_COMMAND: out COLUMN_NUM);



procedure DO_COMMANDS (TEXT_MODE  : out MODE;
                       INDENTATION: out INDENT_RANGE) is

   -- This procedure handles a sequence of command lines.

   NEXT_COMMAND: COMMAND_INFO;
   LINE_COUNT  : ARG_RANGE;

begin
   while NEXT_INPUT_CHAR = COMMAND_CHAR and MORE_DATA(SOURCE_TEXT) loop
      PARSE_LINE (NEXT_COMMAND);

      case NEXT_COMMAND.NAME is
         when PARAGRAPH => TEXT_MODE := PARGRAPH_MODE;
         when VERBATIM  => TEXT_MODE := VERBATIM_MODE;
         when INDENT    => INDENTATION := NEXT_COMMAND.ARGUMENT;
         when CENTER    => for LINE_COUNT := 1 to NEXT_COMMAND.ARGUMENT loop
                              CENTER_LINE;
                           end loop;
         when SPACE     => for LINE_COUNT := 1 to NEXT_COMMAND.ARGUMENT loop
                              START_NEW_LINE;
                           end loop;
         when PAGE      => FINISH_PAGE;
         when ILLEGAL   => PRINT_MARGIN (ERROR_MARGIN);
                           PRINT_TEXT (NEXT_COMMAND.LINE);
                           START_NEW_LINE;
      end case;
   end loop;
end;
```

Example 12.1   continued

```
    procedure PARSE_LINE (COMMAND: out COMMAND_INFO) is

      -- This procedure parses a command line and checks the
      -- legality of any given argument.

      LINE          : LINE_INFO;
      NAME          : COMMAND_NAME;
      ARGUMENT      : ARG_RANGE;
      END_OF_COMMAND: COLUMN_NUM;

begin
   GET_LINE (LINE);
   GET_COMMAND (LINE, NAME, END_OF_COMMAND);

   if (NAME = PARAGRAPH or NAME = VERBATIM or NAME = PAGE)
   and LINE.LENGTH /= END_OF_COMMAND then
      NAME := ILLEGAL;
   end if;
   if NAME = INDENT or NAME = CENTER or NAME = SPACE then
      GET_ARGUMENT (LINE, END_OF_COMMAND, NAME, ARGUMENT);
      if NAME = INDENT and ARGUMENT > RIGHT_MARGIN then
         NAME := ILLEGAL;
      elsif NAME /= ILLEGAL then
         COMMAND.ARGUMENT := ARGUMENT;
      end if;
   end if;

   COMMAND.LINE := LINE;
   COMMAND.NAME := NAME;
end;
```

Example 12.1   continued

```
procedure CENTER_LINE is

   -- This procedure handles an input line that is to be centered, and
   -- prints an error message if the line is too long or is a command.

   LINE             : LINE_INFO;
   LEADING_BLANKS : INTEGER;
   NEXT_CHAR        : CHARACTER;
   IS_COMMAND_LINE: BOOLEAN;

begin
   if MORE_DATA(SOURCE_TEXT) then
      if NEXT_INPUT_CHAR = COMMAND_CHAR then
         IS_COMMAND_LINE := TRUE;
      else
         IS_COMMAND_LINE := FALSE;
      end if;
      while NEXT_INPUT_CHAR = BLANK and MORE_ON_LINE(SOURCE_TEXT) loop
         GET_CHAR (NEXT_CHAR);
      end loop;
      GET_LINE (LINE);

      if LINE.LENGTH > 0 then
         if LINE.LENGTH < RIGHT_MARGIN then
            LEADING_BLANKS := (RIGHT_MARGIN - LINE.LENGTH) / 2;
         else
            LEADING_BLANKS := 0;
         end if;
         if IS_COMMAND_LINE or (LINE.LENGTH > RIGHT_MARGIN) then
            PRINT_MARGIN (ERROR_MARGIN);
         else
            PRINT_MARGIN (NORMAL_MARGIN);
         end if;
         DO_INDENT (LEADING_BLANKS);
         PRINT_TEXT (LINE);
      end if;
      START_NEW_LINE;
   end if;
end;
```

Example 12.1   continued

```
      procedure GET_ARGUMENT (LINE          : in LINE_INFO;
                              END_OF_COMMAND: in COLUMN_NUM;
                              NAME          : in out COMMAND_NAME;
                              ARGUMENT      : out ARG_RANGE) is

   -- This procedure determines the value of an argument given with a
   -- command line. An illegal argument is reported as an illegal command.

   COLUMN   : COLUMN_NUM;
   NEXT_CHAR: CHAR;

begin
   if END_OF_COMMAND = LINE.LENGTH then
      if NAME = CENTER or NAME = SPACE then
         ARGUMENT := 1;
      else
         NAME := ILLEGAL;
      end if;
   else
      COLUMN := END_OF_COMMAND + 1;
      while LINE.IMAGE(COLUMN) = BLANK loop
         COLUMN := COLUMN + 1;
      end loop;
      NEXT_CHAR := LINE.IMAGE(COLUMN);

      if NEXT_CHAR not in '0'..'9' then
         NAME := ILLEGAL;
      else
         ARGUMENT := DIGIT_VALUE(NEXT_CHAR);
         if COLUMN /= LINE.LENGTH then
            COLUMN := COLUMN + 1;
            NEXT_CHAR := LINE.IMAGE(COLUMN);

            if (COLUMN /= LINE.LENGTH) or NEXT_CHAR not in '0'..'9' then
               NAME := ILLEGAL;
            else
               ARGUMENT := ARGUMENT*10 + DIGIT_VALUE(NEXT_CHAR);
            end if;
         end if;
      end if;
   end if;
end;
```

Example 12.1   continued

```
procedure GET_COMMAND   (LINE            : in LINE_INFO;
                         NAME            : out COMMAND_NAME;
                         END_OF_COMMAND: out COLUMN_NUM   ) is
   -- This procedure analyses a command line and determines
   -- the kind of command.

   MAX_COMMAND_LENGTH: constant INTEGER := 10;
   COMMAND_STRING    : STRING(1 .. MAX_COMMAND_LENGTH);
   BREAK_FOUND       : BOOLEAN;

begin
   BREAK_FOUND     := FALSE;
   END_OF_COMMAND := 0;

   for COLUMN := 1 to 10 loop
      if (COLUMN > LINE.LENGTH) or BREAK_FOUND then
         COMMAND_STRING(COLUMN) := BLANK;
      elsif LINE.IMAGE(COLUMN) = BLANK then
         COMMAND_STRING(COLUMN) := BLANK;
         BREAK_FOUND            := TRUE;
      else
         COMMAND_STRING(COLUMN)  := LINE.IMAGE(COLUMN);
         END_OF_COMMAND := END_OF_COMMAND + 1;
      end if;
   end loop;

   if    COMMAND_STRING = ":PARAGRAPH" then
      NAME := PARAGRAPH;
   elsif COMMAND_STRING = ":VERBATIM " then
      NAME := VERBATIM;
   elsif COMMAND_STRING = ":INDENT   " then
      NAME := INDENT;
   elsif COMMAND_STRING = ":CENTER   " then
      NAME := CENTER;
   elsif COMMAND_STRING = ":SPACE    " then
      NAME := SPACE;
   elsif COMMAND_STRING = ":PAGE     " then
      NAME := PAGE;
   else
      NAME := ILLEGAL;
   end if;
end;
```

Example 12.1   continued

```
- - - - - - - - - - - - -

with GLOBAL_DEFINITIONS, UTILITY_ROUTINES;
package body TEXT_ROUTINES is
   use GLOBAL_DEFINITIONS, UTILITY_ROUTINES

   procedure GET_WORD    (WORD: out LINE_INFO);
   procedure PRINT_WORD (WORD        : in LINE_INFO;
                         INDENTATION: in IDENT_RANGE;
                         COLUMN      : out COLUMN_NUM);




procedure DO_VERBATIM (INDENTATION: in INDENT_RANGE) is

   -- This procedure handles one or more verbatim lines.

   LINE     : LINE_INFO;
   NEW_LENGTH: INTEGER;

begin
   while NEXT_INPUT_CHAR /= COMMAND_CHAR and MORE_DATA(SOURCE_TEXT) loop
      GET_LINE (LINE);

      if LINE.LENGTH > 0 then
         NEW_LENGTH := LINE.LENGTH + INDENTATION;

         if NEW_LENGTH > RIGHT_MARGIN then
            PRINT_MARGIN (ERROR_MARGIN);
         else
            PRINT_MARGIN (NORMAL_MARGIN);
         end if;
         DO_INDENT (INDENTATION);
         if NEW_LENGTH > MAX_LINE_LENGTH then
            LINE.LENGTH := LINE.LENGTH - (NEW_LENGTH - MAX_LINE_LENGTH);
         end if;
         PRINT_TEXT (LINE);
      end if;

      START_NEW_LINE;
   end loop;
end;
```

Example 12.1 continued

```
procedure DO_PARAGRAPH (INDENTATION: in INDENT_RANGE) is

   -- This procedure handles one or more paragraph lines, taking
   -- account of new paragraphs and deleting extra space between words.

   PARAGRAPH_INDENT   : constant INTEGER := 5;
   WORD               : LINE_INFO;
   COLUMN, NEW_INDENT: COLUMN_NUM;
   NEW_PARAGRAPH      : BOOLEAN;

begin
   COLUMN := INDENTATION;
   NEW_PARAGRAPH := TRUE;

   while NEXT_INPUT_CHAR /= COMMAND_CHAR and MORE_DATA(SOURCE_TEXT) loop
      GET_WORD (WORD);
      if WORD.LENGTH = 0 then -- blank line found
         if COLUMN /= INDENTATION then  -- close off last line
            NEW_LINE;
            COLUMN := INDENTATION;
         end if;
         NEW_PARAGRAPH := TRUE;
         START_NEW_LINE;
      else
         while WORD.LENGTH /= 0 loop
            if NEW_PARAGRAPH then
               COLUMN := COLUMN + PARAGRAPH_INDENT;
               NEW_IDENT := INDENTATION + PARAGRAPH_INDENT;
               PRINT_WORD (WORD, NEW_INDENT, COLUMN);
               NEW_PARAGRAPH := FALSE;
            else
               PRINT_WORD (WORD, INDENTATION, COLUMN);
            end if;
            GET_WORD (WORD);
         end loop;
      end if;
      CLOSE_OUT_LINE;
   end loop;
   if COLUMN /= INDENTATION then
      START_NEW_LINE;
end;
```

Example 12.1 continued

```
procedure GET_WORD (WORD: out LINE_INFO) is

   -- This procedure reads in the next word of a paragraph.

   BLANK_CHAR: CHAR;

begin
   while (NEXT_INPUT_CHAR = BLANK) and MORE_ON_LINE(SOURCE TEXT) loop
      GET_CHAR (BLANK_CHAR);
   end loop;

   WORD.LENGTH := 0;
   while NEXT_INPUT_CHAR /= BLANK and MORE_ON_LINE(SOURCE_TEXT) loop
      if WORD.LENGTH < MAX_LINE_LENGTH then
            WORD.LENGTH := WORD.LENGTH + 1;
            GET_CHAR (WORD.IMAGE(WORD.LENGTH));
      end if;
   end loop;
end;
```

Example 12.1   continued

```
procedure PRINT_WORD (WORD       : in LINE_INFO;
                      INDENTATION: in INDENT_RANGE;
                      COLUMN     : in out COLUMN_NUM) is

   -- This procedure prints the next word in a paragraph,
   -- attempting to fill a line as much as possible.

   FIRST_WORD_ON_LINE: BOOLEAN;
   END_OF_WORD       : INTEGER;

begin
   if COLUMN = INDENTATION then
      FIRST_WORD_ON_LINE := TRUE;
      END_OF_WORD        := COLUMN + WORD.LENGTH;
   else
      FIRST_WORD_ON_LINE := FALSE;
      END_OF_WORD        := COLUMN + WORD.LENGTH + 1;
   end if;
   if not FIRST_WORD_ON_LINE and (END_OF_WORD > RIGHT_MARGIN) then
      -- won't fit on current line
      START_NEW_LINE;
      COLUMN := INDENTATION;
      FIRST_WORD_ON_LINE := TRUE;
      END_OF_WORD := INDENTATION + WORD.LENGTH;
   end if;

   if END_OF_WORD > MAX_LINE_LENGTH then
      -- is first word on line and still won't fit
      WORD.LENGTH := WORD.LENGTH - (END_OF_WORD - MAX_LINE_LENGTH);
      PRINT_MARGIN (ERROR_MARGIN);
      DO_INDENT (INDENTATION);
      PRINT_TEXT (WORD);
      START_NEW_LINE;
   else
      if FIRST_WORD_ON_LINE then
         PRINT_MARGIN (NORMAL_MARGIN);
         DO_INDENT (INDENTATION);
      else
         PRINT_TEXT (BLANK);
      end if;
      PRINT_TEXT (WORD);
      COLUMN := END_OF_WORD;
   end if;
end;
```

Example 12.1 continued

INDEX